P9-CCN-001

ESSENTIALS
of the Dodd-Frank Act

ESSENTIALS SERIES

The Essentials Series was created for busy business advisory and corporate professionals. The books in this series were designed so that these busy professionals can quickly acquire knowledge and skills in core business areas.

Each book provides need-to-have fundamentals for those professionals who must:

- Get up to speed quickly, because they have been promoted to a new position or have broadened their responsibility scope
- Manage a new functional area
- Brush up on new developments in their area of responsibility
- Add more value to their company or clients

Other books in this series include:

For more information on any of the above titles, please visit www.wiley.com.

ESSENTIALS
of the Dodd-Frank Act

Sanjay Anand

WILEY

John Wiley & Sons, Inc.

Copyright © 2011 by Sarbanes-Oxley Group. All rights reserved.

Published by John Wiley & Sons, Inc., Hoboken, New Jersey.

Published simultaneously in Canada.

No part of this publication may be reproduced, stored in a retrieval system, or transmitted in any form or by any means, electronic, mechanical, photocopying, recording, scanning, or otherwise, except as permitted under Section 107 or 108 of the 1976 United States Copyright Act, without either the prior written permission of the Publisher, or authorization through payment of the appropriate per-copy fee to the Copyright Clearance Center, Inc., 222 Rosewood Drive, Danvers, MA 01923, (978) 750-8400, fax (978) 646-8600, or on the web at www.copyright.com. Requests to the Publisher for permission should be addressed to the Permissions Department, John Wiley & Sons, Inc., 111 River Street, Hoboken, NJ 07030, (201) 748-6011, fax (201) 748-6008, or online at http:// www.wiley.com/go/permissions.

Limit of Liability/Disclaimer of Warranty: While the publisher and author have used their best efforts in preparing this book, they make no representations or warranties with respect to the accuracy or completeness of the contents of this book and specifically disclaim any implied warranties of merchantability or fitness for a particular purpose. No warranty may be created or extended by sales representatives or written sales materials. The advice and strategies contained herein may not be suitable for your situation. You should consult with a professional where appropriate. Neither the publisher nor author shall be liable for any loss of profit or any other commercial damages, including but not limited to special, incidental, consequential, or other damages.

For general information on our other products and services or for technical support, please contact our Customer Care Department within the United States at (800) 762-2974, outside the United States at (317) 572-3993 or fax (317) 572-4002.

Wiley also publishes its books in a variety of electronic formats. Some content that appears in print may not be available in electronic books. For more information about Wiley products, visit our web site at www.wiley.com.

Library of Congress Cataloging-in-Publication Data:

Anand, Sanjay, 1969- author.
  Essentials of the Dodd-Frank Act/Sanjay Anand.
    p. cm. — (Essentials Series)
  Includes index.
  ISBN 978-0-470-95233-7 (pbk.): ISBN 978-1-118-02831-5 (ebk);
ISBN 978-1-118-02832-2 (ebk); ISBN 978-1-118-02833-9 (ebk)
    1. United States. Dodd-Frank Wall Street Reform and Consumer Protection Act. 2. Financial services industry—Law and legislation—United States. 3. Financial institutions—Law and legislation—United States. I. Title.
    KF969.58201A2 2011
    346.73'082—dc22

                                                                    2010047242

Printed in the United States of America.

10 9 8 7 6 5 4 3 2 1

To my son

Contents

Foreword

Great business leaders share many common positive attributes, such as intellectual curiosity and a propensity to act. In periods of significant business transformation, consummate business leaders step out even further to train and explain new business and regulatory developments to the masses.

I met Sanjay Anand at the beginning of last decade's massive regulatory overhaul, triggered by the passage of the Sarbanes-Oxley Act of 2002 (SOX). This swift legislative reaction to major corporate and accounting scandals, at Enron and other companies, caused those at publicly held companies to scramble in an attempt to grasp the compliance requirements for their organizations. Sanjay stepped up with his book, *Essentials of Sarbanes-Oxley* (John Wiley & Sons, 2007), which provided actionable information for those responsible for implementing SOX. I reviewed and commented on his book, and witnessed his commitment to professional development with his subsequent books and the many courses sponsored by his SOX Institute.

In the aftermath of the 2008 credit crisis and related economic downturn, once again Sanjay Anand has stepped forward to lead and explain the Dodd-Frank Wall Street Reform and Consumer Protection Act of 2010 (Dodd-Frank Act) in this book.

It is crucial that everyone in business and proportionally every "consumer" understand this new and far-reaching law of the land. The Act is extensive, but even more significant are the expected regulations that will follow. Unlike earthquakes, where aftershocks diminish as time passes, the flow of regulations from the Dodd-Frank Act is anticipated to be considerable and ever expanding.

Dodd-Frank addresses too-big-to-fail bailouts and includes recommendations for risk committees at certain financial institutions. It gives the Federal Deposit Insurance Corporation (FDIC) powers to "disaffirm or repudiate any contract or lease to which the covered financial institution is a party" and recover or clawback compensation in certain circumstances. The Act expands bounties for whistleblowers and gives shareholders some "say on pay." These are revolutionary changes of epic proportions!

For the consumer, the Dodd-Frank Act establishes a new independent watchdog agency within the Federal Reserve to make sure consumers receive clear and accurate information regarding financial products' terms and costs. It creates a consumer hotline, a new office of financial literacy, and generally expands accountability for consumer protection.

As a business executive and board member whose business foundation is as a CPA, I clearly see how important it is to update laws in order to meet modern-day business conditions and velocities. It is incumbent on all business owners and managers, and indeed all consumers, to understand the Dodd-Frank Act. More important, as a business manager and director, I call on readers to get involved in helping to shape the regulations that are certain to follow from this new law. Too much regulation—or the wrong kind of regulation—can be a drag on businesses and the economy.

Dodd-Frank is also significant in that it implements the first amendments to SOX. Who better to provide insights on Dodd-Frank than Sanjay Anand, who was among the first responders of consummate business leaders to explain SOX? You have chosen wisely, and I know you will greatly benefit from reading this book.

Michael P. Cangemi, CPA

Michael P. Cangemi, CPA, an author and business advisor, is the former president, chief executive officer, and director of Etienne Aigner Group, Inc., a leading designer of women's accessories (1991–2004), and president, chief executive officer, and director of Financial Executives International, the professional association for senior-level corporate financial executives (2007–8). He currently serves as president of Cangemi Company LLC. Mr. Cangemi recently completed a two-year term on the International Accounting Standards Board Standards Advisory Council and a year as the FEI representative on the board of COSO. For more information see www.canco.us.

Preface

On July 21, 2010, President Barack Obama signed into law the Dodd-Frank Wall Street Reform and Consumer Protection Act (Dodd-Frank Act; this Act is also often referred to as DFA, SOX II, the Sequel, Financial SOX, F-SOX, and other variants of these), arguably the most significant financial reform legislation enacted since the Securities Act of 1933 and the Securities Exchange Act of 1934. Just as those Depression-era pieces of legislation were crafted in response to the Great Crash of 1929, the Dodd-Frank Act grew out of what is termed the Great Recession of 2008.

At 848 pages, the final length of the Dodd-Frank Act (H.R. 4173) is considerably shorter than the 2,000-plus pages hyped by the media, yet its length and complexity far surpass the 66-page Sarbanes-Oxley Act of 2002 and the 37-page Glass-Steagall Act of 1933. Many have argued that the incremental repeal of various provisions of Glass-Steagall, such as removing the wall between investment and depository banks, sowed the seeds of the 2008 crisis—a series of events that brought our globally interwoven financial system to the brink of collapse.

Just as Sarbanes-Oxley was created to increase the transparency of and accountability within publicly traded companies, the intention of the Dodd-Frank Act was to unravel the tangled web of financial service company valuations—valuations that were all too often obscured by complex and opaque financial instruments. The introduction of H.R. 4173 on December 2, 2009, was a reaction to having witnessed banks, ratings agencies, insurance companies, accounting firms, and hedge funds serve up a toxic stew of tainted assets and liabilities that reeked of systemic non-disclosure.

As with Sarbanes-Oxley, critics have charged that the Dodd-Frank Act was hastily assembled and rammed through Congress as a short-term fix, absent consideration of its long-term consequences. Although at press time, regulators are still in the process of sorting through its requirements, creating new agencies, and seeking public comment on various regulatory provisions, it is clear that the Dodd-Frank Act will represent a sea change in the way financial services companies—from debt collection agencies to too-big-to-fail banks—conduct their governance, risk management, and compliance activities. As such, the Dodd-Frank Act of 2010 must be understood, accommodated, and mastered in order to integrate regulatory requirements with business objectives.

To stay up-to-date with the Dodd-Frank Act as it evolves from here, visit www.TheDoddFrankAct.com.

Acknowledgments

First and foremost, I would like to thank the publisher, John Wiley & Sons, for reaching out to me to write this book on a current and critical topic, a piece of legislation that is likely to reshape the financial system of not just the United States but the rest of the world as well.

Due to the tight deadline given by the publisher, I would also like to thank my wife and my son for the sacrifices they had to make due to my hectic schedule and long nights before the computer researching, writing, and editing the manuscript.

I am also grateful to my colleagues Arun Kumar and Leema Adam for their assistance in the research and writing, without which this book would not be possible, and to Sally Smith for her perspectives and edits.

I am grateful to Financial Executives International (FEI)'s past chief executive and president, Michael P. Cangemi, CPA, for his endorsement of this book through a foreword.

Finally, I thank you, the readers, who have placed your trust in this book to provide you with the information you need as you embark on your journey toward compliance with the Dodd–Frank Wall Street Reform and Consumer Protection Act.

CHAPTER 1

Introduction to the Dodd-Frank Act

The Dodd–Frank Act represents a new regulatory landscape for the financial services industry. As with any newly enacted legislation, it is imperative that organizations quickly get up to speed regarding both the broad strokes and the nuances of the law. When you stay ahead of the curve, you can anticipate your organization's need for new compliance initiatives, adjust your risk management framework to ensure that you do not run afoul of the law, and prepare your corporate governance structure and corporate culture to align with both the letter and the spirit of the law.

This book will provide you with the roadmap for this new landscape. By presenting both the big picture and the details of the Dodd–Frank Act, it better prepares you to lead your organization through a path of compliance and risk mitigation.

We begin with the genesis of the Dodd–Frank Act, examining the events that led up to its introduction, the key players involved, and a review of the legislation's timeline. From there, we take each of the Act's 16 titles and probe their meanings and implications:

- **Title I** of the Act addresses systemic risk of the economic system and creates two new governmental agencies: the Financial Stability Oversight Council and the Office of Financial Research. The goal of the Financial Stability Oversight Council is to identify systemic risks, promote market discipline, and respond to emerging threats. The purpose of the Office of Financial Research is to provide support to the Council through administrative, technical, and analytical means.

- **Title II** addresses the orderly liquidation of insolvent financial companies, some of which were already covered by the Federal Deposit Insurance Corporation (FDIC) or Securities Investor Protection Corporation (SIPC), and others—such as insurance companies—and provides for the creation of the Orderly Liquidation Fund, to be funded by certain financial companies.

- **Title III** abolishes the Office of Thrift Supervision, dispersing its powers among the Federal Reserve, the FDIC, and the Office of the Comptroller of the Currency. It also permanently increases the maximum amount of deposits insured by the FDIC and includes provisions for ensuring ethnic and gender diversity within financial regulatory agencies.

- **Title IV** adds reporting requirements for investment advisors and seeks to increase transparency. It also mandates three studies, two from the Government Accountability Office (GAO) (on defining "accredited investor" and self-regulation for private funds) and one from the Securities and Exchange Commission (SEC) (on short selling and related reporting).

- **Title V** creates the Federal Insurance Office within the U.S. Treasury to monitor the insurance industry, administer the Terrorism Insurance Program, and identify regulatory gaps that could lead to a financial crisis. It also includes a smattering of consumer protections as well as a mechanism to allocate premium taxes to individual states.

- **Title VI** addresses the Volcker Rule, which creates a "church and state" separation between banking and other types of financial services, such as hedge funds and private equity funds. It also calls for greater disclosure of proprietary trading and increased capital requirements.

- **Title VII** regulates over-the-counter swaps and repeals the regulation exemption that existed under the Gramm-Leach-Bliley Act. In addition, the title directs the Commodity Futures Trading Commission, the SEC, and the Federal Reserve to define security swap terms and mandates the creation of a group to oversee the carbon market, spot markets, and derivative markets.

- **Title VIII** grants the Federal Reserve more authority with regard to systemic risk by requiring it to create uniform standards for risk management for too-big-to-fail financial institutions and to strengthen the liquidity of market utilities.

- **Title IX** includes a number of investor protections and mandates a variety of studies. It creates the Office of the Investor Advocate, mandates the SEC to develop point-of-sale disclosure rules for investors, and provides for a whistleblower reward program. In addition, it gives the SEC broad power to regulate shareholder proxy materials and withhold information gathered by oversight activities. Further, it regulates asset-backed securities, requires publicly held companies to garner shareholder approval for and disclose executive compensation, and mandates disclosure of incentive-based compensation.

- **Title X** creates an independent Bureau of Consumer Protection under the auspices of the Federal Reserve and is tasked with five broad objectives: research, community affairs, complaint tracking, fair lending, and financial literacy.

- **Title XI** amends the Federal Reserve Act, giving the president authority to appoint, subject to Senate confirmation, the New York Federal Reserve president, and creating the position of vice chairman for supervision on the Board of Governors. It also includes provisions for the GAO to audit the Federal Reserve and requirements for the Federal Reserve to create standards (such as risk management and capital requirements) for institutions under their supervision.

- **Title XII** authorizes incentives that can be used by a variety of organizations to encourage those who do not utilize mainstream financial services to do so. It creates programs to conduct activities such as microloans, financial education, and getting low- and moderate-income people to open accounts in FDIC-insured banks.

- **Title XIII** reduces the funds available to the Troubled Asset Relief Program and amends the Housing and Economic Recovery Act of 2008, Emergency Economic Stabilization Act of 2008, and the American Recovery and Reinvestment Act of 2009.

- **Title XIV** contains a number of consumer protections related to mortgages and lending. It regulates mortgage originators, establishes a semblance of underwriting standards for residential loans, defines "high-cost mortgages," establishes an Office of Housing Counseling within the Department of Housing and Urban Development, amends the Real Estate Settlement Procedures Act, defines property appraisal requirements, and tasks the Department of Housing and Urban Development with designing a mortgage resolution and modification program.

- **Title XV** includes a number of miscellaneous provisions relating to everything from mine safety and the International Monetary Fund to natural resource licensing and the effectiveness of Inspectors General.

- **Title XVI** redefines marked to market trades in Section 1256 contracts to exclude derivatives and futures contracts or options other than dealer securities future contracts.

After delving into each title of the Dodd-Frank Act, we move into the kind of actionable information that you need in order to move forward. We cover the effective dates and rule promulgation deadlines that you need to have handy as well as outlining the institutions impacted by the Act. From there, we review related legislation and rulemaking that could impact your industry and your organization, such as the Truth in Lending Act, the Fair Credit Reporting Act, and the Investment Advisers Act.

Then, after a summary of the roles of new and existing governmental agencies as defined by the Act, we analyze the global impact and implications of the Act for the banking and investment industries.

Next, we offer valuable advice for professionals impacted by the Dodd-Frank Act, including those involved with executive management, municipal securities markets, and broker-dealers.

Finally, we examine the Dodd-Frank Act's relationship to the Sarbanes-Oxley Act of 2002 (SOX) as well as its relationship to the Basel Accords. After all, newly minted legislation often leaves imprints on the statutes that preceded it and sometimes has unintended consequences. If your organization is required to be SOX compliant, it is crucial to understand how the Dodd-Frank Act will impact your compliance initiatives.

Although this book is written primarily for senior-level professionals, executives, and board members in the financial services and legal professions, it will also be useful to those in other disciplines, such as accounting, audit, information technology, and ethics. Like SOX, the Dodd-Frank Act will affect those at every organizational level, from the chief executive to middle management and beyond. This book seeks to impart information to anyone who may be impacted by the Act, both to prepare for the regulations that will inevitably follow and to create a roadmap for implementing specific titles and sections of the Act within organizations.

CHAPTER 2

History and Background

After reading this chapter, you will be able to

- Understand the events that led to the passage of the Dodd–Frank Wall Street Reform and Consumer Protection Act.
- Grasp the scope of the Dodd–Frank Act.
- Recognize Christopher Dodd and Barney Frank, the architects of the Act.
- Understand the timeline during which the legislation was crafted and enacted.
- Pinpoint the key goals of the Act.

The Dodd–Frank Wall Street Reform and Consumer Protection Act (Dodd–Frank Act) is a federal statute that was signed into law by President Barack Obama on July 21, 2010. Before signing the Act, President Obama remarked that although many factors influenced the severity of the recession, the primary cause of the breakdown of the U.S. financial system was the failure of responsibility from certain corners of Wall Street and the halls of power in Washington.[1] President Obama stated that the old and poorly enforced laws had facilitated a few to take risks that endangered the entire U.S.

economy. This setback in the rules helped them take advantage of the financial system.

In 1933, the National Industrial Recovery Act (NIRA) was signed by President Franklin D. Roosevelt. Although the Act was unable to contribute much to the economy, it was still considered to be a major financial sector takeover by the U.S. government at that time. Until the Dodd-Frank Act, no other legislation had attempted such a large-scale financial reform. The Dodd-Frank Act brings many changes to the legislation that supervises the financial industry and is one of the most ambitious regulated reforms that has governed the financial industry since the Great Depression era.

The Dodd-Frank Act is the product of the financial regulatory reform agenda of the 111th U.S. Congress. The Act was first proposed on December 2, 2009, in the House by Chairman Barney Frank and in the Senate Banking Committee by Chairman Chris Dodd. This Act has the capacity to affect every single financial institution and commercial company in the country. It focuses on both large and small financial institutions, but the regulations imposed on small institutions have relatively expensive frameworks. The Act also affects both domestic and foreign financial institutions.

The passage of the Act shifted the approach of commercial companies and financial institutions toward banking, derivatives, securities, private equity funds, credit rating agencies, debit card interchange fees, consumer protection, executive compensation, and corporate governance.

Financial Instability

The Dodd-Frank Act was an initiative taken by the U.S. government to reform the disorders that resulted from the Great Recession of 2008. The recession caused a collapse of the stock market, higher levels of borrowings in the credit market, escalation of oil prices due to geopolitical uncertainties, more hidden risks in hedge funds, insufficient flow of capital, an increase in unemployment, and a rise in the United States' foreign debts and deficits in its current accounts.

The markets became inefficient due to the complexity of the information shared with investors and lack of transparency. Too many financial organizations offered risky products. Companies focused more on short-term profits than on the long-term interests of their shareholders. Executive compensation, which was topping the graphic scale, was mostly unjustifiable. There was an overall failure of capitalism in the U.S. stock markets and economy.

Bank depositors' money was used for proprietary trading. Commercial institutions sold risky loans in markets separate from where they sold prime loans and public company executives participated in risk-prone activities. There was underfunding even in the cases of pension obligations. The derivatives market saw multiple complexities. The procedures involved in clearings, settlements, and the evaluations of risks and instruments administration were not managed properly and suitably.

Scope

The U.S. government realized that the economic bust was caused by the failure of capitalism and the inefficiency of previously passed regulations. The first step was to bring about financial reform by recognizing the factors causing problems and then finding ways to solve them. The Dodd-Frank Act was proposed to address the causes that brought market failure.

The Act has a wide scope. Its regulations help stabilize the economy by constant supervision of the financial sector. It aims to reduce and eliminate the systemic risks that threaten the stability of the country's economy.

The Act objectively cuts across globally interconnected financial companies. It carefully reminds regulators of the capabilities and the capacities at which they are required to work. It mandates regulatory controls that insist on transactional transparency and highlights the importance of investor information that could possibly provide safe havens in high-risk situations.

In short, the Dodd-Frank Act seeks to stabilize a vital segment of the country's economy through regulatory frameworks. The frameworks supervise the working of newer markets and protect investors, markets, and consumers. The Act also has an international effect due to the interconnectedness of economies.

Architects of the Dodd-Frank Act

The Dodd-Frank Act was proposed on December 2, 2009. House Financial Services Committee chairman Barney Frank (D-MA), introduced the bill in the White House and Senator Chris J. Dodd (D-CT), the chairman of the Senate Banking Committee, introduced a similar bill in the Senate Banking Committee. Their similar Federal Housing Administration (FHA)–based plans aimed to support the distressed mortgage markets and the unstable housing markets. A conference committee met on June 29, 2010, and voted to name the bill the Dodd-Frank Act.

After President Obama signed the bill on July 21, 2010, Senator Dodd issued a press release stating:

> With this bill, we have protected taxpayers from being forced to bail out companies that threaten to bring down the economy. With new consumer protections the government will no longer sit idly by as consumers fall victim to scams by credit card companies and mortgage giants. After today, regulators will no longer be able to ignore emerging threats to the economy. And financial operators from the trillion dollar derivatives market to small time payday lending will no longer be able to operate in the shadows.[2]

Both Frank and Dodd have responded to the recession and credit crunch by incorporating a number of effective tools that borrowers and lenders have used to recover from the instability of the financial situation. Their initiative in finding as many specific targeted solutions as possible is also worth noting.

The Plan and Proposal

At the time the Dodd-Frank Act was proposed, the economy was in need of a reform that would foster innovation. The Act was intentionally designed so that everyone follows the same set of rules. It also enables firms to compete on price and quality.

Addressing a critical area of the economy, the Dodd-Frank plan aimed to bring existing mortgage prices below face value in order to make them more affordable. After reducing these mortgage prices, the federal government, rather than a big bank, would act as the insurer. However, the government's duty is not to solely assume the risk of default.

It was anticipated that, since the resale mortgage markets would be virtually shut down when current market values are below face values, the government would be required to synthesize a resale market for mortgages until the reemergence of a real one. Mortgage servicers act as intermediaries between homeowners and mortgage owners. Congress was compelled to pass legislation that would protect these servicers from legal liability when market conditions worsened.

The Dodd-Frank plan proposed that none of its emergency measures should last longer than the emergency. For example, the plan had provisions to facilitate FHA mortgages to be packaged, securitized, and resold into the market as soon as feasible conditions emerged. After a few years, the Act would end the FHA mortgage grants. Both Frank and Dodd stressed the importance of setting upper limits on family incomes and house values when it came to mortgages and discouraged less onerous requirements. In other words, mortgages with complex terms and structure are encouraged, thereby raising the bar on qualifications required to obtain a mortgage especially for the high-end of the marketplace.

With all the required components set in place, President Obama finalized and signed the bill, which included 90% of the initial proposal components. The only component added later was the Volcker Rule, which was passed in January 2010. Some of the proposal's components are:

- Consolidation of financial regulatory entities
- Elimination of national thrift charter
- Evaluation of systemic risk by new oversight council
- Regulation of financial markers
- Increased transparency of the derivatives in financial markets
- Newer consumer protection reforms
  - Consumer protection agency with newer horizons
  - Uniform standardization
  - Strong investor protection criteria
- Tools required to rescue in times of crisis
- Measures to tighten credit rating agency regulation and to improve international standards, cooperation, and accounting

The Volcker Rule states that only 3% of a bank's tangible common equity can be invested in hedge funds or private equity. It also states that proprietary trading at bank holding companies is not allowed.

The House of Representatives passed the bill on June 30, 2010, with a vote of 237 to 192.[3] The Senate passed the bill on July 15, 2010, with a vote of 60 to 39, allowing the bill to become law.

Timeline

Here is a look at the passage of legislative events that led to the enactment of the Dodd-Frank Act.

Date	Event
December 2, 2009	Bill introduced
December 11, 2009	Bill passed by the House of Representatives
May 20, 2010	Bill passed by the Senate with amendment
June 30, 2010	Conference committee created to work out differences between the Senate and House version bills
July 15, 2010	Differences resolved
July 21, 2010	Bill signed by President Obama

The Dodd-Frank Bill is the longest bill passed in the history of the United States' financial regulation. It is believed that this Act will be able to mitigate the results of any crisis that may arise in the future.

Key Goals of the Act

The Dodd-Frank Act is a major piece of legislation that affects the banking and financial sectors. The Act is considered one of the biggest legislative takeovers approved by Congress. The law does not give new power or rights to banks and financial service companies but instead designs new regulations for these institutions to address issues that are results of the recent recession. This restrictive measure prevents the recurrence of similar financial disasters in the future. This law serves as a safety net to the financial markets in the United States.

The Act's primary motive is "to promote the financial stability of the United States by improving accountability and transparency in the financial system, to end 'too big to fail,' to protect the U.S. taxpayer by ending bailouts, to protect consumers from abusive financial services practices, and for other purposes."[4]

The Act intends to change banking and securities legislation. It has the capacity and capability to change the operational methods of many institutions and persons, including:

- Banks
- Mortgage businesses

- Hedge funds
- Thrifts
- Insurance companies
- Industrial loan companies and their parent companies
- Credit rating agencies
- Public companies
- Bank, financial, savings, and loan holding companies
- Investment adviser firms
- Attorneys who advise these entities
- Broker-dealers
- Accountants

The Dodd-Frank Act promotes confidence in the economy by putting into place a system that is financially accountable and transparent. It works for the benefit of the entire U.S. community and also aims to protect it at times of critical need.

The Act applies to both large financial firms and small practitioners' offices and affects their day-to-day operations without partiality. This law has international implications and sets standards to enable the implementation of the Act and regulate it without disruption. It has a wide scope and consists of 16 distinct titles on a diverse spectrum of economic matters.

Summary

- The Dodd-Frank Wall Street Reform and Consumer Protection Act is a federal statute that was signed into law by President Barack Obama on July 21, 2010.
- The Dodd-Frank Act was enacted in response to systemic failures that led to the Great Recession.

- The Act: consolidates financial regulatory entities; provides a mechanism for evaluation of systemic risk; creates new consumer protection reforms; regulates financial markers, credit rating agencies, and derivatives; and limits banks' investments in hedge funds and private equity.

- The Act impacts a wide range of financial services companies as well as consumers, and has international implications.

- The Act has a broad scope and is comprised of 16 distinct titles.

Notes

1. "Obama's Remarks at Signing of Dodd-Frank Wall Street Reform and Consumer Protection Act," July 21, 2010, Council on Foreign Relations Publications. www.cfr.org

2. "President Signs Dodd-Frank Wall Street Reform Bill," July 21, 2010, Chris Dodd, United States Senator for Connecticut. http://dodd.senate.gov/?q=node/5725

3. H.R. 4173: Dodd-Frank Wall Street Reform and Consumer Protection Act, updated July 24, 2010. http://docs.house.gov/rules/finserv/111_hr_finsrv.pdf

4. Dodd-Frank Wall Street Reform and Consumer Protection Act – The SEC www.sec.gov/about/laws/wallstreetreform-cpa.pdf.

CHAPTER 3

Key Titles and Sections

After reading this chapter, you will be able to:

- Understand the membership and function of the Financial Stability Oversight Council.

- Grasp the new powers granted to the Federal Reserve Board.

- Understand the role of the Office of Financial Research.

- Recognize how the Dodd-Frank Act provides for the orderly liquidation of financial institutions.

- Understand the variety and scope of studies required by the Dodd-Frank Act.

- Understand the process of dismantling the Office of Thrift Supervision.

- Understand the scope of and exemptions to the Private Fund Investment Advisers Registration Act of 2010.

- Understand the functions of the Federal Insurance Office.

- Grasp the regulatory changes for depository institutions and depository institution holding companies, including the Volcker Rule.

- Understand the regulatory frameworks for over-the-counter and security-based swap markets.

- Recognize changes to financial market payments, payment clearing, and settlement systems.
- Understand the Securities and Exchange Commission's Office of Credit Ratings and Investor Advisory Committee.
- Understand the role of the new Bureau of Consumer Financial Protection.
- Comprehend restrictions to the Federal Reserve Board's emergency lending ability.
- Understand how the Dodd-Frank Act encourages improved access to mainstream financial institutions by low- and moderate-income consumers.
- Grasp the revisions to the Troubled Asset Relief Program (TARP).
- Understand new anti-predatory requirements for mortgage lenders.
- Understand the Dodd-Frank Act implications for those investing in derivative contracts.

Title I: Financial Stability

Title I establishes the Financial Stability Oversight Council (FSOC). This council of regulators will monitor the financial system for systemic risk and will also determine the components that would cause systemic risk. The title recommends the implementation of standardized risk regulators, which are also known as prudential regulators. Prudential regulators will be applied to bank holding companies with a total consolidation of assets valued at $50 billion or more. These are applied to nonbank financial companies also.

Along with large bank holding companies, the title enables systemic identification of the "nonbank financial companies" for heightened regulation by the Federal Reserve. The Federal Reserve's policy on small bank holding companies was also preserved. Title I grants powers to the Federal Reserve Board (FRB) to implement prudential standards for large interconnected bank holding companies and nonbank financial companies supervised by the Board of Governors.

Title I also creates the Office of Financial Research (OFR). This office collects, analyzes, and shares information. Both the FSOC and the OFR are attached to the U.S. Treasury Department. The secretary of the Treasury chairs the council while a presidential appointment with the Senate's confirmation heads the OFR.

The FSOC and FRB are invested with the power to request information from companies to determine their systemic significance. Title I aims at mitigating the risks that arise as a result of activities of large interconnected firms by making them abide by this Act's stringent regulatory framework. As a result, the financial stability of the U.S. market is also secure.

This title also includes the Collins Amendment, which mandates that federal banking agencies establish new, and sometimes higher, minimum-leverage and risk-based capital requirements. The Collins Amendment also imposes minimum capital requirements on insured depository agencies, their holding companies, and systemic nonbanks. This amendment was aimed primarily at minimizing or eliminating the use of hybrid capital instruments, which could help in the regulatory capital requirement compliance of financial institutions.

The Act administers trust preferred securities issued by bank holding companies having less than $15 billion in total assets value before May 19, 2010. Trust preferred securities that are the permissible components of the Tier I capital, with certain exceptions, will be eliminated through this amendment.

Financial Stability Oversight Council

The FSOC was established with the passage of the Dodd-Frank Act. The council consists of ten voting members and five nonvoting members. The FSOC identifies and responds to potential risks that threaten the financial stability of the United States. The FSOC is also involved in promoting a disciplinary regime in the financial market.

In addition, the FSOC monitors domestic and international proposals. The council facilitates the sharing of information with regulatory agencies. The FSOC provides recommendations to the Federal Reserve Board when it comes to prudential standards and also has the capacity to designate nonbank financial companies as systemically significant. The FSOC maintains confidentiality over the information that it collects and receives. The council does not demand any waiver on the information it receives and does not affect the privileges to the information that are already in application.

The FSOC has the power to collect information from nonbank financial companies. Through this process, it determines whether these companies should be subjected to prudential supervision. Sometimes the FSOC may require systemic bank holding companies or systemic nonbanks to submit reports. These reports must clearly elaborate on the financial conditions of the companies and their capacity to disrupt the stability of the financial markets and, henceforth, the U.S. economy at times of adversity.

The secretary of this council also serves as chairperson and has voting rights. The FSOC must meet at least once every three months and at the announcement of the council's secretary. Issues are decided based on the majority of votes. Sometimes, critical matters involving enhanced regulations of specific firms or activities are decided upon the voting strength of a two-thirds majority. This majority must include a "yes" from the council's chairperson.

Members of the FSOC

Listed next are the voting and nonvoting members of the FSOC.

Voting Members	Nonvoting Members
Chairperson of FSOC	Director of Office of Financial Research
Comptroller	Director of Federal Insurance Office
Independent member*	State Insurance Commissioner
Chairman of Federal Reserve Board	State Banking Supervisor[†]
Chairman of Securities and Exchange Commission	State Securities Commissioner[†]
Chairman of National Credit Union Administration	
Director of the Bureau of Consumer financial Protection	
Director of Federal Housing Finance Agency	
Chair of Federal Deposit Insurance Corporation	
Chairman of Commodities Future Trading Commission	

*The independent member will serve a six-year term and should be an expert in insurance.
[†]Each of these members will serve a term of two years in office.

Office of Financial Research

The OFR is established by Title I of the Dodd-Frank Act. The OFR consists of a data center and a research and analysis center. The data center is responsible for data collection, while the research and analysis center helps analyze the data and monitor the systemic risk.

The title specifies that for the first two years, the OFR would be funded by the FRB. After two years, the office will continue to function with the fee collected for its services to the systemic bank holding companies and systemic nonbanks.

The OFR helps the FSOC accurately collect and analyze information. This processed information is given to the FSOC or member agencies. The OFR specializes in developing tools to monitor and measure risks and provides information to the financial regulatory agencies. The

OFR has the power to subpoena and acquire the information or report it requires. This office also helps agencies determine the types and forms of data authorized by the Dodd-Frank Act. With this assistance, the financial regulatory agencies are able to collect the required data.

Systemically Significant Institutions

The concept of "systemically significant" institutions is an important one in the context of financial regulation. In the paragraphs that follow, we identify the systemically significant institutions, the role that they play, and the impact of the Dodd-Frank Act on them.

U.S. Nonbank Financial Companies

The FSOC subjects U.S. nonbank financial companies to FRB supervision and prudential standards by its voting result. A nonbank financial company is engaged in financial activities if 85% or more of the consolidated annual gross revenues or assets are results of activities of financial nature and if it owns an insured depository institution.

A U.S. nonbank financial company that is notified by the FSOC of a possible designation as a systemic nonbank will have 30 days to contest the intention of designation by the FSOC. Anything determined by the FSOC at the last minute is subject to judicial review at the U.S. District Court for the District of Columbia or the U.S. District Court in the district where the nonbank company's home office is located. The review is limited; the court judges decide whether the FSOC's determination is illogical and impulsive. Even with the use of this review, it is very difficult to overturn the determination of the FSOC.

The nonfinancial activities of a systemic nonbank are not listed as the nonbanking activities by the Bank Holding Company Act (BHCA). But the FRB requires that the financial activities be placed in an intermediary holding company, which is subject to the BHCA.

First, the FRB creates regulations to determine when a nonbank financial company's financial activities should be placed in an intermediate holding company. Following this, the FRB treats the intermediate company as a nonbank, and any commercial activities placed in the top tier are not subject to FRB supervision.

Foreign Nonbank Financial Companies

The FSOC determines if a foreign nonbank financial company should be subjected to FRB supervision by a two-thirds majority vote. Along with size, scope, and various other factors, the company's presence in the United States is also taken into consideration. The FSOC follows a similar set of regulations to that of the domestic nonbank financial company to designate a foreign nonbank as systemic.

The Dodd-Frank Act details the factors that confirm a company as a foreign nonbank. The first factor is that the company must be organized under the laws of a country other than the United States. The company also should not be a bank holding company or a subsidiary of a bank holding company. Second, the company should be predominantly engaged in activities with a financial nature. The foreign nonbank company can request a hearing to contest the FSOC's intention to designate it as systemic.

The FSOC may require a foreign nonbank financial company to establish an intermediate holding company just as in the case of a U.S. nonbank financial company. The foreign nonbank financial company has 180 days to register with the FRB after it is designated as a systemic nonbank.

U.S. Bank Holding Companies

The Dodd-Frank Act has prudential requirements for bank holding companies and states that a bank holding company with a consolidated

asset worth $50 billion is subjected to prudential standards as a systemic
bank holding company. The FSOC and FRB may establish a threshold
above $50 billion for the prudential requirements application. This does
not include risk-based capital, risk management, leverage requirements,
liquidity requirements, or stress testing.

Foreign Bank Holding Company

Non-U.S. banks or non-U.S. companies that are bank holding companies, either because of their U.S. bank ownership or because they
operate a U.S. branch or agency, are treated as systemic bank holding companies by the Dodd-Frank Act when their consolidated
assets are valued at $50 billion or more. The Act does not specify
whether this is applicable to the company's assets in the United
States.

Prudential Standards

The FSOC is required to recommend prudential standards, while
the Federal Reserve Board is required to implement them. These
prudential standards help avoid or minimize the risks that threaten
the financial stability of the United States. The standards applicable
to the systemically significant institutions vary in stringency according to the risk factors. Based on the FSOC's recommendation, the
FRB may establish certain prudential standards for companies with a
consolidated asset value at $50 billion or more. Neither the FSOC
nor the FRB is restrictive in applying the prudential standards to
firms according to situations.

The FSOC must give special consideration to the principles of national treatment, equality of competitive opportunity, and the foreign
company's adherence to the home country's standards before subjecting
it to prudential requirements.

Areas of Prudential Standards

It is mandatory for the FSOC to establish prudential standards in risk-based capital and leverage limits, liquidity requirements, overall risk management, resolution plans, credit exposure reporting, and concentration limits. In addition, the FRB can establish the prudential standards in other areas, such as contingent capital, enhanced public disclosures, and short-term debt limits. It may establish any other prudential standards when it deems appropriate. These standards include:

- **Risk-based capital and leverage limits.** The title requires regulatory agencies to establish minimum capital requirements for all insured depository institutions and their holding companies. The FRB has to adopt risk-based capital and leverage limits and impose a 15:1 leverage ratio on systemically designated companies. The FSOC must conduct a study to analyze the establishment of contingent capital requirement for systemic nonbanks and systemic bank holding companies.

- **Liquidity requirements.** These liquidity requirements are likely to be based on the general principles of the Interagency Policy Statement on Funding and Liquidity Risk Management, which were set out on March 17, 2010.

- **Risk management.** The FRB mandates that a systemically designated company establish a risk committee within one year of systemic determination. The risk management committee will be responsible for the risk management practices of the company. The risk committee must include independent directors as stipulated by the FRB, as well as a risk management expert.

- **Resolution plans.** The systemically significant companies must submit a plan to the FSOC, the FRB, and the FDIC. This plan should help make the resolution of the company rapid and orderly at the time when it is at material financial distress or failure. The plan is otherwise known as a living will. The FSOC and the FDIC have 18 months to issue final implementation rules for this section from the date of Dodd–Frank Act's enactment.

- **Concentration limits, credit exposure.** Credit exposure includes all credit extensions, credit exposure under repurchase agreements, securities lending arrangements, guarantees, other credit enhancements, investment in company's securities, and other derivatives transactions. The systemic institutions must prepare a credit exposure report identifying the potential exposures of the company's counterparties to the FSOC and the FDIC. The report's regulations are guided by the Interagency Guidance on Correspondent Concentration Risk as of April 30, 2010. The effective date is three years after the date of enactment, with a possible two-year extension if approved by the FRB.

- **Enhanced public disclosures.** This supports the systemically significant company to evaluate market and acquire risk profile, capital adequacy, and risk management capabilities.

- **Short-term debts.** Liabilities that mature within a short time are short-term debts. These liabilities are identified by the FRB. The FRB must limit the short-term debt amount, including off balance sheet exposures.

Collins Amendment

The Collins Amendment aims to reduce or eliminate the use of hybrid capital instruments, such as trust preferred securities. The amendment requires that many changes be made to the current regulatory capital regime applicable to all bank holding companies and thrift holding companies. The Collins Amendment mandates heightened requirements for systemic entities, fixed leverage limits for certain companies, and a contingent capital study.

With this amendment, holding companies with less than a $15 billion asset value continue to include existing trust preferred securities in Tier I capital. Holding companies with a $15 billion or more asset value do not include trust preferred securities in Tier I capital for a certain period of time. The Government Accountability Office (GAO) must conduct a study to analyze the use of hybrid capital instruments as a Tier I capital component and then must report the result to Congress within 18 months of the enactment of the Dodd-Frank Act.

Protecting the Financial System

The FSOC recommends that financial regulatory agencies apply new standards to any activity or practice that could create or increase instability in the financial system. When a systemically significant company poses a grave threat to financial stability, the FRB requires the company to immediately terminate one or more activities, impose conditions on the manner in which the company conducts its activities, and restrict the offer of financial products. The FRB also sets a limitation on the merging and acquisition of the companies. If these recommendations fail to mitigate the threat, the FRB then recommends that the systemic company sell or transfer the assets of off–balance sheet items to unaffiliated entities.

The FRB is compelled to conduct an annual stress test of systemically significant companies. The test offers to consider situations that are categorized as baseline, adverse, and severely adverse. The systemic companies will also have to conduct an internal stress test on a semi-annual basis. All other financial companies with assets of more than $10 billion that are supervised by the federal regulatory agency should conduct an annual stress test.

The FRB prescribes certain early remediation requirements to systemic companies. The company will have to define its financial condition measures and must establish stringent measures that would increase its efficiency if the financial condition of the company deteriorates.

Under the Depository Management Interlocks Act, a systemic nonbank is treated as a systemic bank holding company. However, the FRB may not permit the dual service performed by the management official of a systemic nonbank with another systemic nonbank or a systemic bank holding company.

If a bank holding company was to debank or cease to be a bank holding company, then the entity should be treated as a systemic nonbank. In order for this to occur, the entity should appeal to the FSOC in a hearing. But the Act does not provide any judicial review of the final determination. If denied, the FSOC must annually review and reevaluate the appeal under this section of the Act. The FRB has the power to impose reporting regulations on systemic companies. The FRB also has vested powers to supervise these systemically significant companies.

The Act encourages other countries to impose similar standards and to discourage regulatory arbitrage opportunities created by jurisdictions with different standards. The FRB is allowed to consider and evaluate whether the home country of a foreign bank that poses a threat to U.S. financial stability has adopted certain standards to mitigate such risks. This Act also allows the Securities and Exchange Commission (SEC) to determine whether a foreign person's home country has adopted standards to mitigate risks in the U.S. financial markets.

Title II: Orderly Liquidation Authority

In addition to the policies and procedures in place for the financial institutions covered by the FDIC and the Securities Investor Protection Corporation (SIPC), this title provides for the orderly liquidation of other financial institutions. Other financial companies that may be liquidated under this title include insurance companies and nonbank financial companies not covered elsewhere.

Once it is determined that a financial company satisfies the criteria for liquidation, and if the financial company's board of directors does not agree, provisions are made for judicial appeal. Some procedures for the FDIC and SIPC to liquidate companies are revised in this title.

Depending on the type of financial institution, different regulatory organizations may jointly or independently, by a two-thirds vote, determine whether a receiver should be appointed for the liquidation of a financial company.

The secretary of Treasury, in consultation with the president, may also make a determination to appoint a receiver for a financial company. The GAO shall review and report the secretary's decision to Congress.

When a financial institution is placed into receivership under these provisions, the secretary shall report to Congress within 24 hours and to the general public within 60 days. The report on the recommendation to place a financial company into receivership shall contain various details on the state of the company, the impact of its default on the company, and the proposed action.

Judicial Review

After the secretary determines that the financial company is "systemic" under the criteria specified in this title, he or she will notify the corporation and the covered financial company. If the board of directors of the company accepts the appointment, the secretary then appoints the corporation as receiver. Otherwise, the secretary will petition the U.S. District Court for authorization to appoint the corporation as receiver.

The secretary will present all relevant findings to the court. After a notice to the covered financial company and a hearing in which the covered financial company may oppose the secretary's petition, the court confidentially determines whether the secretary's determination is valid.

If the court finds that the determination of the secretary is valid, the court then authorizes the secretary to appoint the corporation as the receiver in case the financial institution is not arbitrary and capricious. If the financial institution is arbitrary and capricious, the court will immediately provide a written statement to the secretary detailing its support for its determination and will advise the secretary to amend and refile the petition.

If the court takes more than a day to determine the petition, the petition will be granted the operation of law. The secretary will appoint the corporation as receiver, and the liquidation process under this title will commence automatically without further notice.

The determination of the court will be final and is not subjected to any stay or pending appeal. The court provides a copy of its written statement supporting its reasons for determination to both the secretary and the covered financial company.

The U.S. Court of Appeals for the District of Columbia has the jurisdiction to make an appeal on the final decision of the court on the petition filed by the secretary. This jurisdiction is effective only if the covered financial company does not accept the appointment of the corporation as the receiver. The review to this appeal is limited, as it checks whether the determination by the secretary of the covered financial company is arbitrary and capricious.

A written petition contesting the decision of the Court of Appeals is filed with the Supreme Court. The Supreme Court has discretionary jurisdiction to review the appeal. The court of appeals will have to submit a written statement on its reasons for the decision. Like the court of appeals, the judicial review of the Supreme Court is also limited.

Powers and Duties of the Corporation

After its appointment by the secretary as the receiver to the covered financial company, the corporation enjoys all rights, titles, powers, assets, stockholders, members, officers, and directors of the company as its successor. The corporation is entitled to maintain the books, records, and assets of the covered company.

During the process of orderly liquidation, the corporation has the authority to take over the assets of and conduct business for the covered financial company. It collects all obligations and monies that are owed to the covered financial company, and it performs all functions in the name of the covered financial company.

The corporation can provide for the functioning of any member, stockholder, director, or officer of the covered financial company for which it has been appointed as the receiver. The corporation is subject to all legally enforceable perfected securities interests and all legally enforceable security entitlements in respect of assets held by covered financial company.

The corporation can be involved in the liquidating and concluding of affairs of a covered financial company according to the manner it deems appropriate. The corporation can sell the assets of the covered financial company or transfer the assets to a bridge financial company.

The corporation can appoint itself as the receiver of a covered subsidiary of a covered financial company. In order to do so, the corporation and the secretary have to jointly determine whether the covered subsidiary is in default and if the actions of the subsidiary could mitigate the stability of the financial system in the United States.

When the corporation appoints itself as the receiver of the covered subsidiary, the covered subsidiary will be treated as a covered financial company. The corporation then has all the powers and rights to the covered subsidiary.

The corporation can organize the bridge financial company, merge the covered financial company with another company, and transfer any asset or liability of the covered financial company without obtaining approval, assignment, or consent. The corporation, to the extent of funds available, shall pay all valid obligations of the covered financial company.

The corporation can exercise all powers and authorities that are specifically vested to it, as receiver under this title. The corporation can utilize the services of private persons and can determine the utilization of such services. It can terminate all rights and claims that a stockholder or creditor may have against the assets of the covered financial company. It can coordinate with the foreign financial authorities regarding the orderly liquidation of any covered financial company.

As receiver of the covered financial company, the corporation can also report on claims. The corporation, at its sole discretion, can pay creditors their claims and dividends on claims. The corporation can request a stay in judicial action or proceeding. It also has the capacity to avoid transfer of any interest of the covered financial company in property, or obligation incurred with the actual intent to hinder, as well as defraud an entity within two years before the date of which the corporation was appointed as receiver.

It has the authority to avoid transfer of interest of covered financial company in property to benefit a creditor, or on account of antecedent debts that was owed by the covered financial company before the transfer, and so forth, the corporation may avoid the transfer of property of the receivership that occurred after the appointment of the corporation as the receiver and hence not authorized by the corporation now, as the receiver.

The corporation is superior to any rights of any trustee or any other party under the bankruptcy code. Any right of a creditor to offset a mutual debt owed by the creditor to any covered financial company, before the appointment of the corporation as the receiver against the claim of such creditor, may be asserted if it is enforceable under the applicable insolvency law.

If a creditor offsets a mutual debt owed to the covered financial company against a claim of the covered financial company on which the corporation is appointed as the receiver, the corporation may recover from the creditor the amount to offset.

At the request of the corporation, any court of competent jurisdiction may issue an order placing the assets of any person designated by the corporation under the control of court and appoint a trustee to hold such assets. Unsecured claims that are proven to the satisfaction.

The corporation has the authority to reject contracts that were entered into before the appointment of the corporation as the receiver for the covered financial company. The corporation appointed as receiver is not liable to punitive damages, damages for lost profit or opportunity, or damages for pain and suffering.

The receiver can reject a lease under which the covered financial company is a lessee and the receiver will not be liable to damages as a result of disaffirmation or repudiation of the lease. If the covered financial company is the lessor and the lessee is not in default, the lessee can terminate the lease.

If the receiver rejects any contract for the sale of real property and the purchaser of such property is in possession and is not in default, that person may terminate the contract. The principle can be applied for service contracts. If the corporation accepts performance but rejects the contract, the other party shall then be paid under the terms of the contract for the services performed.

The corporation cannot avoid certain transfers. It may not avoid any transfer of money or other property in connection with any qualified financial contract with the covered financial company. Other than an insurance contract, the corporation as the receiver of covered financial company has the authority to enforce any contract.

With the approval of the secretary, the corporation can make additional payments of credit; additional amounts of such payments minimize losses to the corporation as the receiver from the orderly liquidation process. The corporation may grant the federal charter to approve the articles of association for one or more bridge financial company or companies. The bridge company will be managed by the board of directors appointed by the corporation.

If permitted by the corporation, the bridge company can elect to follow corporate governance and can function with or without capital or surplus as the corporation sees fit.

The corporation may transfer any asset or liability of a covered financial company to one or more bridge companies according to the restrictions placed. The corporation shall be treated as the sole shareholder in the case of a merger or consolidation. Following sale of majority, the corporation may amend the charter of the bridge financial company. If the bridge company is unable to obtain unsecured credit or issue unsecured debt, the corporation may then authorize the issue of debt or acquisition of credit by the bridge company.

The corporation will make records for a covered financial company on its appointment. The corporation manages the orderly liquidation fund that is established by Title II of the Dodd-Frank Act. A prefunded orderly liquidation fund is not a provision in the legislation. The corporation has the capacity to authorize the funding for the liquidation of a covered financial company, borrowing from the Treasury.

Before the borrowing, the Treasury and the SIPC must execute an agreement with a specific plan. This plan must show the income from the liquidated assets of the covered financial company. The corporation and Treasury must submit a copy of the repayment schedule to Congress within 30 days of its receipt of funding from the corporation.

The corporation may periodically submit a request for reimbursement for implementation expenses. The corporation may impose on covered financial companies the collection of information requirements. The corporations may prescribe rules to carry out the regulations.

Miscellaneous Provisions

The inspector general of the corporation shall conduct, supervise, and coordinate audits and investigations of liquidation. An evaluation of the overall performance of the corporation in liquidating is completed. The inspector general of the corporation will include this evaluation and testify in the semiannual reports. The expenses of the inspector general of the corporation are treated as administrative expenses.

The inspector general of the Treasury will conduct, supervise, and coordinate the audits and examinations done by the secretary in relation to liquidation. The inspector general of the Treasury will submit a summary of findings and assessments in the semi-annual reports.

The inspector general of the financial regulatory agency will submit written reports after reviewing the supervision done by the agency or the board of directors of the covered financial company.

Ban on Certain Activities by Senior Executives and Directors

If the Board of Governors or the corporation determines that a senior executive or a director of the covered financial company, prior to the appointment of the corporation as receiver, has:

- Violated
  - Any law or regulation
  - Any cease-and-desist order
  - Any written agreement between such company and such agency
  - Any condition imposed in writing by a federal agency in connection with any action, notice, application, or request
- Engaged or participated in any unsafe or unsound practice in connection with any financial company
- Committed or engaged in any act, omission, or practice which constitutes a breach
- Received any financial gain or other benefit by reason such violation, practice or breach
- Such violation, practice, or breach involves personal dishonesty or for the safety or soundness of such company

The agency can then take the following authorized actions:

- Send a written notice of the intention of the agency to prohibit such person from participating in the financial affairs of the company.
- Determine the period of time that the senior executive or director is prohibited, with the period of time not being less than two years.

Prohibition on Taxpayer Funding

All financial companies that are subjected to receivership shall be liquidated under this title. Taxpayer funds cannot be used to prevent the liquidation of any financial company. All funds spent on the liquidation process shall be recovered from the disposition of assets of that particular financial company. The taxpayers are not subjected to any loss when this title is exercised.

Studies

The Dodd-Frank Act mandates that the following studies be conducted, and the reports that are results of these studies should be submitted to Congress.

Study on Secured Creditor Haircuts

- The FSOC shall conduct a study evaluating the importance of maximizing U.S. taxpayer protections and promoting market discipline with respect to the treatment of fully secured creditors in the utilization of the orderly liquidation authority authorized by this act.
- In carrying out the study, the Council shall:
  - Not be prejudicial to secured creditor treatment with respect to current or past laws or regulation
  - Study the similarities and differences between the resolution mechanisms authorized by the Bankruptcy Code, the Federal Deposit Insurance Corporation Improvement Act of 1991, and the orderly liquidation authority authorized by this Act

- Determine how various secured creditors are treated and examine how a haircut (of various degrees) on secured creditors could improve market discipline and protect taxpayers.

- Compare the benefits and dynamics of secured loan lending practices by depository institutions to consumers and small business versus large and interconnected financial firms.

- Consider whether, based on the types of collateral and terms, credit differs for the extension of credit.

- Report should be submitted within one year from the date of enactment of this Act.

Study on Bankruptcy Process for Financial and Nonbank Financial Institutions

- The Administrative Office and the Comptroller General of the United States will monitor the activities of the court. Each office shall:

  - Conduct a separate study about the bankruptcy and orderly liquidation process for financial companies

  - Evaluate the effectiveness of chapter 7 or 11 of the Bankruptcy Code for orderly liquidation or for reorganization of financial companies

  - Find ways to maximize the efficiency and effectiveness of the Court

  - Find ways to make the orderly liquidation process under the Bankruptcy Code for financial companies more effective

- Reports are to be submitted to Congress within one year after the enactment date of this Act for three successive years. After this period of time, reports are to be submitted every fourth year from the date of enactment.

Study of International Coordination Relating to Bankruptcy Process for Nonfinancial Companies

- The Comptroller General of the United States shall conduct a study regarding international coordination relating to the orderly liquidation of financial companies under the Bankruptcy Code. The Comptroller General will evaluate:
  - The extent to which international coordination currently exists
  - Current mechanisms and structures for facilitating international cooperation
  - Ways to increase and make more effective international coordination
- A report should be submitted to the Committee on Banking, Housing, and Urban Affairs of the Senate and the Committee on Financial Services of the House of Representatives on actions taken in response to the report within one year after the enactment of this act.

Study of Prompt Corrective Action Implementation by the Appropriate Federal Agencies

- The Comptroller General of the United States shall evaluate:
  - The effectiveness of prompt corrective action taken by the appropriate federal banking agencies
  - Ways to make prompt corrective action a more effective tool to resolve the insured depository institutions
- A report should be submitted within one year after the enactment of this Act.
- The Council shall submit a report to the Committee on Banking, Housing, and Urban Affairs of the Senate and the Committee on Financial Services of the House of Representatives on actions taken in response to the report within six months after the receipt of the report.

FDIC and Receivership

The FDIC's appointment as receiver may terminate in three years. The term can be extended by one year if the FDIC provides Congress with a reason for such an extension in writing. With certain limitations, this extension period can be used for completing litigations with the FDIC as receiver. The FDIC may appoint itself as the receiver of any covered subsidiary if it is appointed as the receiver of a covered financial company.

The covered financial subsidiary must be in default or in danger of default before the FDIC and Treasury jointly approve of the appointment. Further appointment should be able to reduce or remove the threats to the financial stability or at least facilitate the orderly liquidation of the covered financial company. Insured depository institutions, insurance companies, or covered brokers and dealers are not covered financial subsidiary.

The orderly liquidation is modeled on the resolution authority under the Federal Deposit Insurance Act (FDIA) for the insured depository institutions. Some of the powers vested on the FDIC allow it to: take over the financial company's assets and operate it, sell the assets or transfer the assets to a bridge financial company, merge the financial company with another company; value and prioritize claims; avoid fraudulent transfers and preferences; prioritize administrative expenses of the receiver; prohibit settlements with secrecy agreements; create and operate bridge financial companies. The FDIC also has many other powers vested on it.

The provisions to the orderly liquidation of the Dodd-Frank Act and the FDIA differ from each other in certain aspects. Regardless, this orderly liquidation process is created to ensure that the private sector bears the cost of the proceeding and the removal of management, and that the responsible parties are held accountable.

Covered Brokers, Dealers, and Insurance Companies

After the appointment of the FDIC as the receiver for the covered broker dealer, the SIPC has to be appointed as a trustee for the brokers-
dealers' liquidation. The SIPC would resume its functions and would
continue to have the powers and duties as specified in the Securities Investor Protection Act. The FDIC has the right to create and operate a
bridge financial company. The bridge financial company should be registered with the SEC and self-regulatory organizations (SROs) and can
operate as broker-dealer in compliance with the securities laws.

The state regulator is responsible for the liquidation of financial
companies that are insurance companies. If the state regulator fails to file
for appropriate judicial action in the state court within 60 days of determination, the FDIC may stand in the place of the state insurance regulator and file the liquidation action in state court.

Repayments

The FDIC manages the orderly liquidation fund that is established by
the second title of the Dodd-Frank Act. A prefunded orderly liquidation
fund is not a provision in the legislation. The FDIC has the capacity to
authorize the funding for the liquidation of a covered financial company, borrowing from the Treasury.

But before the borrowing, the Treasury and the Securities Investor
Protection Corporation must execute an agreement with a specific plan.
This plan must show the income from the liquidated assets of the covered financial company. The FDIC and Treasury must submit a copy of
the repayment schedule to Congress within 30 days of its receipt of
funding from the FDIC.

Apart from this, the Dodd-Frank Act requires studies on secured
creditor haircuts, bankruptcy processes for financial and nonbank financial institutions, and international coordination relating to bankruptcy

process for nonbank financial institutions to be conducted, with the result being submitted to Congress.

The general provisions of Title II of the Dodd–Frank Act are effective one day after the enactment of this Act. Hence, the orderly liquidation is immediately available, should a systemic financial institution experience financial instability.

Title III: Transfer of Powers to the Office of Comptroller of the Currency, Corporation, and Board of Governors

Title III enhances the safety and sound operations of financial institutions and ensures that fair and appropriate supervision exists for each depository institution and its holding companies.

This provision eliminates the Office of Thrift Supervision (OTS) and gives its powers to the Office of Comptroller of the Currency (OCC), the FDIC, and the Board of Corporations. This title also makes certain changes to the FDIC by increasing the standard maximum deposit insurance amount to $250,000.

Transfer of Powers and Duties

The transfer of powers from the OTS occurs within one year from the date of enactment of the Act, and an extension of another six months is also possible. The regulators should issue regulations to new companies as soon as the powers are transferred. The OTS will cease to exist, and its employees will become the employees of the OCC or the FDIC 90 days after the transfer of powers and duties is complete.

Although it was initially proposed to eliminate the thrift charter, the Dodd–Frank Act only abolishes the OTS and transfers its powers to the OCC, the FDIC, and the FRB. The OCC acts as OTS's successor in regulating federal thrift. Although a separate thrift division is not established, the specially appointed deputy comptroller supervises and examines the federal thrifts.

Transfer of OTS Functions to Corporations (FDIC)

All functions of the OTS related to "state savings associations" are transferred to the corporation.

Transfer of OTS Functions to Comptroller of the Currency

All functions and rulemaking authority relating to "federal savings associations" and "savings associations" are transferred to the OCC. The OCC will succeed to all the powers, authorities, rights, and duties that were vested with OTS.

Transfer of OTS Functions to Board of Governors

Functions and rulemaking authority for savings and loan holding companies and their subsidiaries are transferred to the Board of Governors (FRB). Thus, the FRB becomes the primary regulator of thrift holding companies and assumes all rulemaking authority of the OTS under Section 11 of the Home Owners Loan Act (HOLA) relating to transactions with affiliates and extensions of credit to executive officers, directors, and principal shareholders, and under Section 5(q) of HOLA, related to tying arrangements.

Abolishment of OTS and transfer date within 90 days after the transfer, OTS, and the positions of directors of OTS are abolished. The transfer of OTS powers will take place one year after the enactment of the Dodd-Frank Act, and it can be extended by six months if required.

By the transfer date, the FRB, the FDIC, and the OCC are required to publish a set of regulations that would be enforced by each of the offices. The FDIC and OCC will have to consult each other on their establishment and enforcement of regulations. Any thrift that converts to bank charter is allowed to the continued operation of branches and agency offices.

The converted thrifts can establish, buy, and operate additional branches within any state where the thrift operated a branch before the thrift charter conversion. The converted thrift is also permitted to retain branches in states where it did not have a branch prior to the enactment of the Gramm-Leach-Bliley Act (GLBA).

Continuation of Existing OTS Orders, Resolutions, and Others

The Dodd-Frank Act provides for the continuation of existing orders, resolutions, determinations, agreements, and so on that were issued prior to the Act by OTS. FRB, OCC and FDIC are required to identify the existing OTS regulations that will be enforced by each agency. FDIC and OCC will identify the regulations that they need to enforce it independently and will publish it in the Federal Register.

Funding

For carrying out the examination of regulated entities, the OCC, the FDIC, and the FRB may collect an assessment, fee, or other charge on the basis as specified below.

OCC. When establishing the amount, these issues must be taken into account: the nature and scope of the activities of the entity, the amount and type of assets that the entity holds, the financial and managerial condition of the entity, and any other factors that OCC determines are appropriate.

FDIC. The cost of conducting any regular or special examination of any depository institution or entities as prescribed in the respective sections may be assessed to meet the expenses of the corporation in carrying out such examinations.

FRB. The board can collect the total amount that is equal to the total expenses that are necessary to carry out the supervisory and regulatory responsibilities from:

All bank holding companies or savings and loan holding companies having total consolidated assets of $50 billion or more.

All nonbank financial companies supervised by the Board under section 113 of the Dodd-Frank Act.

Transfer of Employees, Properties, and Funds

Title III gives elaborate processes and procedures for the transfer of employees from OTS to OCC, FDIC, and FRB. Some of the highlights are:

- Employee will hold the same status and tenure.
- No additional certification is required before placing employees in the respective departments.
- 30-month protection of pay from the transferred date.
- Continuation of existing retirement plan.
- Special provision to ensure continuation of life insurance benefits.
- Equitable treatment of employees after the transfer.

All property and contracts related to the property of the OTS must be transferred to OCC and FDIC in a manner consistent with the transfer of employees no later than 90 days after the transfer date.

Personal property, such as books, accounts, records, reports, files, memoranda, papers, documents, reports of examination, work papers, and correspondence, are transferred between OCC, FDIC, and FRB based on each organization's functions.

Funds in OTS before the transfer date are distributed among OCC, FDIC, and FRB based on their functions as defined in Section 312.

Implementation Plan and Reports

Within 180 days of the enactment of the Dodd-Frank Act, the Board of Governors, the Corporation, the OCC, and OTS shall jointly submit a plan detailing the steps that will be taken to implement the provisions of sections 301 through 326 to the Committee on Banking, Housing, and Urban Affairs of the Senate, the Committee on Financial Services of the House of Representatives, and inspectors general of the Department of the Treasury.

Within 60 days of receiving the plan, the respective agencies will review whether the plan takes into consideration:

- The orderly transfer of personnel, authority, and responsibilities
- The effective transfer of funds
- The orderly transfer of property

The implementation report is monitored every six months until the plan is fully implemented.

Federal Deposit Insurance Corporation

The Act impacts existing roles and responsibilities of the FDIC. In particular, it affects the following key areas:

Deposit Insurance

The FDIA is amended to make a permanent increase in the deposit insurance amount from $100,000 to $250,000. This increase covers depositors in any institution for which the FDIC acts as the receiver on or after January 1, 2008, and before October 3, 2008. Organizations such as Indy Mac Bank and FSB, and uncovered depositors are primarily benefited by this increase in coverage. This provision is scheduled to expire on December 31, 2013.

Share Insurance

The share insurance also increased from $100,000 to $250,000.

Non–Interest-Bearing Transaction Account

If a deposit is maintained in an insured depository institution, then the full deposit insurance coverage extends for non–interest-bearing transaction accounts for the net amount.

Definition given to a non–interest bearing transaction account is listed:

- The interest is neither accrued nor paid.
- Depository institution does not reserve the right to require advance notice of an intended withdrawal.
- Depositor or account holder is permitted to withdraw by negotiable or transferable instrument, or through telephone or electronic media for making payments or transfers to third parties or others.

Assessment Base

For the insured depository institution, the revised assessment base is set to an amount equal to the average consolidated total assets of the insured depository institution during the assessment period, minus the average tangible equity during the assessment period. If the insured depository institution is a custodial bank or banker's bank, then the corporation determines the amount consistent with the definition under Section 7(b)(1) of the FDIA.

Minimum Reserve Ratio

The Dodd-Frank Act increases the minimum reserve ratio from 1.15% to 1.35% of estimated deposits or the comparable percentage of the assessment base as explained above. The corporation shall take such steps as necessary to reach 1.35% of estimated deposits by September 30, 2020. The FDIC shall offset the effect of minimum reserve ratio on insured depository institutions with a total consolidated asset value of $10 billion. The intent is to charge higher FDIC insurance premiums on bigger banks.

Elimination of Procyclical Assessment

The FDIC is provided with discretionary authority to suspend or limit rebates to insured depository institutions when the reserve ratio exceeds 1.5% of estimated insured deposits. Initially, the FDIA permitted rebates when the reserve ratio margined between 1.35% and 1.5%. The Dodd-Frank Act has now eliminated this provision.

Other Matters

In addition to the agencies and aspects just listed, the Act also has an impact on other important areas. In particular, it addresses minorities and women.

Offices of Minority and Women Inclusion

The legislation requires the establishment of an office for minority and women inclusion in each bank regulatory agency. The offices are responsible for developing standards and procedures to facilitate minority and women inclusion and to encourage minority- and women-owned businesses in agency contracting activities.

Title IV: Regulation of Advisers to Hedge Fund and Others

The Dodd-Frank Act introduces the Private Fund Investment Advisers Registration Act of 2010 to bring in certain exempted private advisers into the umbrella of registration and reporting. It provides limited exemptions from registration under this Act to:

- Foreign private advisers
- Private fund advisers
- Venture capital fund advisers

The Private Fund Investment Advisers Registration Act of 2010 also requires record keeping among the private advisers.

Elimination of Private Adviser Exemption

This Act eliminates Section 203(b) of the Investment Advisers Act of 1940, which earlier exempted private advisers from registration if:

- They had fewer than 15 clients for the previous 12 months.
- They do not act as an investment adviser to the general public.
- They do not act as investment advisers to any registered investment company or business development company.

Limited Exemption and Reporting

The Act stipulates limited exemption of and reporting by the following advisers.

Venture Capital Fund Advisers

The Dodd-Frank Act contains an exemption from registration for investment advisers to venture capital funds. Investment advisers who solely advise to one or more venture capital funds are also exempted. The SEC will issue the definition of the term "venture capital funds" after the first year of the Act's enactment. The SEC will require the investment advisers to maintain such records and provide records and annual or other reports to the SEC for protecting the public interest or for the protection of investors.

Private Fund Advisers

If an investment adviser solely acts as the investment adviser to private funds and manages assets with a value less than $150 million in the United States, registration is exempted. The SEC requires the investment advisers to maintain such records and provide to the SEC annual or other reports to safeguard public interest and protect investors.

Mid-Sized Private Fund Advisers

If the investment adviser manages assets between the values of $25 million and $100 million, he or she may be exempted from registration. If the investment adviser manages assets with a value of more than $25 million and is registered with 15 or more states, then the investment adviser may have to register with the SEC. The SEC has to determine whether such funds pose systematic risk to the investors.

Foreign Private Advisers

The Dodd-Frank Act exempts foreign private advisers from registration with the SEC. The term "foreign private adviser" means any investment adviser who:

- Has no place of business in the United States.

- Has, in total, fewer than 15 clients in the United States.

- Has aggregate assets under management of clients with a value that is less than $25 million.

- Neither holds him- or herself out generally to the public in the United States as an investment adviser nor acts as an investment adviser to any investment company registered with the SEC in the United States.

Commodity Trading Advisers

An investment adviser who is registered with the Commodities Future Trading Commission (CFTC) as a commodity trading adviser and is involved in advising private funds is also exempted from registration with the SEC. If the adviser provides securities-related advice after the date of enactment of the Private Fund Investment Advisers Registration Act of 2010, then the adviser will have to register with the SEC.

Small Business Investment Companies

An investment adviser is exempted from registration if he or she does not advise a company that has elected to be regulated as a business development company and who solely advises:

- Small business investment companies that are licensees under the Small Business Investment Act (SBIA) of 1958.
- Entities that have received from the Small Business Administration (SBA) notice to proceed to qualify for a license as a small business investment company under the SBIA of 1958, which notice or license has not been revoked.
- Applications that are affiliated with one or more licensed small business investment companies and that have applied for another license under the SBIA, and its application remains pending.

Collection of Systemic Risk Data, Reports, Examinations, and Disclosures

The Commission may require any registered investment adviser to keep records, files, and reports regarding the private funds advised by the investment adviser. This is necessary in the interest of public and to safeguard the investors. The Council may ask the investment adviser to provide these records when it requires.

Investment advisers should maintain the details of each private fund with a description of:

- The amount of assets under management and use of leverage, including off-balance-sheet leverage
- Counterparty credit risk exposure
- Trading and investment positions
- Valuation policies and practices of the fund
- Types of assets held
- Side arrangements or side letters, whereby certain investors in a fund obtain more favorable rights or entitlements than other investors
- Grading practices
- Such other information that the Commission, in consultation with the Council, may request

The Commission may conduct periodic or special inspections of the records of private funds maintained by an investment adviser. The Council shall maintain confidentiality of all such reports, documents, records, and information.

Custody of Client Accounts

Registered investment advisers shall take such steps to safeguard client assets over which such advisers have custody, including, without limitation, verification of such assets by an independent public accountant as prescribed by the Commission.

Accredited Investor Standard

Current net worth fixed for an accredited investor is $1 million, excluding the value of primary residence of such natural person or joint net worth with the spouse of that person. The Act directs the SEC to periodically review the definition of "accredited investor."

Studies

Study on Custody Rule Costs

The Comptroller General of the United States shall conduct a study of the compliance costs associated with the current SEC rules regarding custody of funds or securities of clients by investment advisers. The study will also include additional costs if rules relating to operational independence were eliminated. The report is to be submitted no later than three years after the date of enactment of this Act.

Study on Accredited Investors

The Comptroller General of the United States shall conduct a study on the appropriate criteria for determining the financial thresholds or other criteria needed to qualify for accredited investor status and eligibility to invest in private funds. The study should be completed no later than three years after the date of enactment of this Act.

Study on Self-Regulatory Organizations for Private Funds

The Comptroller General of the United States shall conduct a study of the feasibility of forming a self-regulatory organization to oversee private funds and submit a report to the Committee on Banking, Housing, and Urban Affairs of the Senate and the Committee on Financial Services of the House of Representatives on the results of such study. The report should be completed no later than one year after the date of enactment of this Act.

Study on Short Selling

The division of Risk, Strategy and Financial Innovation of the Commission shall conduct a study on short selling with particular attention to the impact of recent rule changes and the incidence of:

- The failure to deliver shares sold short.

- Delivery of shares on the fourth day following the short sale transaction the feasibility, benefits, and costs of requiring reporting publicly, in real time short sale positions of publicly listed securities, or, in the alternative, reporting such short positions in real time only to the Commission and the Financial Industry Regulatory Authority.

Title V: Insurance

This title establishes the Federal Insurance Office (FIO) within the Treasury and also defines its powers and responsibilities. The FIO reviews the insurance industry and the regulations of the Office for the Congress.

The scope of the FIO extends to all areas except health insurance, most long-term care insurance, and crop insurance. The FIO will be responsible for collecting information, monitoring the insurance industry, and providing recommendations to modernize insurance regulations. The FIO can anticipate conflicts in the state laws.

The Dodd-Frank Act tries to create national uniformity in two areas: nonadmitted insurance market and reinsurance.

Federal Insurance Office

The FIO is established within the Department of the Treasury. The office is headed by the director, who is appointed by the secretary of the Treasury.

Functions

The FIO has the authority to:

- Monitor all aspects of the insurance industry and identify issues or gaps in the regulation of insurers that could create a systemic crisis in the insurance industry.

- Monitor the traditionally underserved communities and consumers, minorities, and low- and moderate-income persons who have access to affordable insurance products except health insurance.

- Recommend to the FSOC to designate an insurer and its affiliates as an entity.

- Assist in administering the Terrorism Insurance Program established in the Department Office.

- Coordinate with other federal and state regulatory agencies before collecting any data or information from an insurer or an affiliate of an insurer to make sure they have the required information.

- Obtain the required information from the insurer or an affiliate if the information is not available from other agencies.

Data collected in the due course has to be maintained under strict confidentiality. The director shall have the power to require, by subpoena, the production of the data or information requested from the insurer or an affiliate. Subpoenas shall bear the signature of the director and shall be served by any person or class of persons designated by the director for that purpose. In case of failure to obey subpoenas, the same can be enforceable in the appropriate district court of the United States. Any failure to obey the order of the court may be punished by the court as a contempt of court.

Preemption of State Insurance Measures

A state insurance measure shall be preempted to this Section or Section 314 if the measure results in less favorable treatment of a non-U.S.

insurer domiciled in a foreign jurisdiction that is subject to a covered agreement than a U.S. insurer domiciled, licensed, or otherwise admitted in that state and is inconsistent with a covered agreement.

Annual Reports

Beginning September 30, 2011, the director shall submit a report on or before September 30 of each calendar year to Congress and the insurance industry. A report on the U.S. and Global Reinsurance Market should be received no later than September 30, 2012, describing the breadth and scope of the market. By January 1, 2015, a report describing the impact of part II of the non-admitted and Reinsurance Reform Act of 2010 should be submitted to the House Financial Service Committee (HFSC) and the Senate Committee on Banking, Housing and Urban Affairs (SBC). The director shall conduct a study and submit a report to Congress on how to modernize and improve the system of insurance regulation in the United States no later than 18 months after the date of enactment of this section.

The report should cover these areas:

- Systemic risk regulation with respect to insurance.
- Capital standards and the relationship between capital allocation and liabilities, including standards relating to liquidity and duration of risk.
- Consumer protection for insurance products and practices, including gaps in state regulation.
- The degree of national uniformity of state insurance regulation.
- The regulation of insurance companies and affiliates on a consolidated basis.
- International coordination of insurance regulation.
- The costs and benefits of potential federal regulation of insurance across various lines of insurance, except health insurance.

- The feasibility of regulating only certain lines of insurance at the federal level, while leaving other lines of insurance to be regulated at the state level.

- The ability of any potential federal regulation or federal regulators to eliminate or minimize regulatory arbitrage.

- The impact that developments in the regulation of insurance in foreign jurisdictions might have on the potential federal regulation of insurance.

- The ability of any potential federal regulation or federal regulator to provide robust consumer protection for policyholders.

- The potential consequences of subjecting insurance companies to a federal resolution authority, including the effects of any federal resolution authority:

  - On the operation of state insurance guaranty fund systems, including the loss of guaranty fund coverage if an insurance company is subject to a federal resolution authority.

  - On policyholder protection, including the loss of the priority status of policyholder claims over other unsecured general creditor claims.

  - In the case of life insurance companies, on the loss of the special status of separate account assets and separate account liabilities.

  - On the international competitiveness of insurance companies.

Negotiating International Insurance Agreements

The Dodd-Frank Act establishes authority for the U.S. Trade Representative (USTR) and the secretary to negotiate covered agreements at the federal level. Before negotiating agreements of international stature, the secretary and the USTR must consult with the HFSC and the SBC and brief them on the nature of the agreements. The agreements are effective only after 90 days of submission to the HFSC and SBC. This time limit is set to action only when Congress is in session.

Non-Admitted Insurance

This title incorporates provisions that increase the market choice for large commercial purchasers to obtain insurance from companies that are not allowed to write insurance in their state. This title comes into force 12 months from the date of enactment of the Dodd-Frank Act.

The term "non-admitted insurance" means any property and casualty insurance permitted to be placed directly or through a surplus lines broker.

The tem "surplus lines broker" means an individual, firm, or corporation that is licensed in a state to sell, solicit, or negotiate insurance on properties or casualty located or to be performed in a state with non-admitted insurers.

Streamlined Application for Commercial Purchasers

A surplus lines broker who wants to procure a non-admitted insurance in a state for an exempt commercial purchaser shall not be required to satisfy any state requirement. The surplus lines broker does not need to make a due diligence effort to search to determine whether the full amount or type of insurance sought by exempt commercial purchaser can be obtained from the admitted insurer if the broker procuring it has disclosed to the exempt commercial purchaser that such an insurance may or may not be available from an admitted market that may provide greater protection with more regulatory oversight, and the exempted commercial purchaser has requested in writing thereafter that the broker produce or places such insurance from a non-admitted insurer.

The exempt commercial purchaser is one who meets these requirements:

- Employs or retains a qualified risk manager to negotiate insurance coverage.
- Is paid in excess of $100,000 toward nationwide commercial property and casualty insurance premiums during the immediately preceding 12 months.
- Meets at least one of the next criteria:
    - **i.** Net worth in excess of $20,000,000.
    - **ii.** Annual revenue in excess $50,000,000.
    - **iii.** Employs more than 500 full-time employees is a member of an affiliated group employing more than 1,000 employees in the aggregate.
    - **iv.** Is a not-for-profit organization or public entity generating annual budgeted expenditures of at least $30,000,000.
    - **v.** Is a municipality with a population in excess of 50,000 persons.
- Effective on the fifth January 1 occurring after the date of the enactment of this subtitle and each fifth January 1 occurring thereafter, the amounts in (i), (ii), and (v) as mentioned above shall be adjusted to reflect the percentage change for such five-year period in the Consumer Price Index for All Urban Consumers published by the Bureau of Labor Statistics of the Department of Labor.

Study of Non-Admitted Insurance Market

The Comptroller General of the United States shall conduct a study of the non-admitted insurance market to determine the effect on this enactment. The study is to analyze and determine:

- The change in the size and market share among the non-admitted insurance and insurance holding companies during the 18-month period from the enactment of this Act.

- How much business was shifted from the admitted insurance market to the non-admitted insurance market.

- The consequences of any change in the size, market share, price or coverage in both the admitted and non-admitted insurance market.

- The shifts in the volume of business between admitted and non-admitted insurance.

- The number of individuals who have non-admitted insurance policies, the type of coverage provided under non-admitted insurance, and whether such coverage is available in the admitted insurance market.

The Comptroller General shall consult with the National Association of Insurance Commissioners (NAIC) for the study and must submit the report to SBC and HFSC within 30 months after the effective date of this act.

Home State Regulation of Non-Admitted Insurance

According to the Act, non-admitted insurance is subject to home state regulations. Specifically, the Act states that:

- Non-admitted insurance is only subject to home state regulation of the insured party.

- Surplus line brokers need to get licensed only in the state where they will sell, solicit, or negotiate non-admitted insurance for the insured party.

- Any attempts by other states to regulate non-admitted insurance activities are preempted with an exception of worker's compensation insurance.

- After two years following the enactment, no states can collect fees relating to the licensing of surplus lines brokers, unless that state is participating in the national insurer database or an equivalent uniform database.

- States are prohibited from imposing eligibility requirements or criteria on U.S.-domiciled, non-admitted insurance.

- States may not prohibit a surplus line broker from placing non-admitted insurance or procuring non-admitted insurance from a non-admitted insurer outside the United States. If the non-admitted insurer is listed on the Quarterly Listing of Alien Insurers maintained by the NAIC.

Premium Tax Payments

Likewise, premium tax payments are subjected to home state regulations as well. In particular:

- Only the home state of an insured party may impose a premium tax on insurance obtained from a non-admitted insurer.

- States may enter into an agreement or otherwise establish procedures to allocate the premium taxes amount to the states.

- For non-admitted insurance, states should adopt a nationwide uniform requirement, forms, and procedures that provide for the reporting, payment, collection, and allocation of premium taxes.

Reinsurance and Reinsurance Agreements

The Dodd-Frank Act has provisions that prevent state law from governing reinsurance arrangements. If the state of residence of an insurer purchasing the reinsurance is NAIC accredited or has financial solvency standards similar to those mandated by the NAIC, the Dodd-Frank Act provides and recognizes credit for reinsurance for the insurer's ceded risk.

After this, no other state may deny such credit for reinsurance. Furthermore, all laws, regulations, or actions of the state where the ceding insurer is not residing, except those states that have to do with taxes, are preempted under Title V of the Dodd-Frank Act.

States that are NAIC credited or have financial solvency requirements are solely responsible for the regulation of financial solvency of reinsures who reside in that state. No state may require a reinsurer to file financial information beyond that which the reinsurer is required to file with its residential state. Nonresiding regulators are allowed to receive copies of filed information.

Title VI: Improvements to the Regulation of Bank and Savings Association Holding Companies and Depository Institutions

Title VI implements various changes in the regulations of depository institutions and depository institution holding companies. The title expands the per-borrower lending limits and adds new limits on the proprietary trading in securities. This is otherwise known as the Volcker Rule.

The Volcker Rule limits the ability of certain bank and bank-related companies to engage in proprietary trading, hedge fund and private equity fund investing up to 3% of the company's Tier I capital. The company faces other restrictions also. It increases the scope of insider trading regulations, insisting on the implementation of new restrictions on thrifts that do not clear the qualified thrift lender test. New rules are laid on dividend waivers by mutual holding companies.

Title VI can provide a suspension to the establishment or acquisition of industrial loan companies, credit card banks, and other nonbanks controlled by commercial companies. It has the authorization of de novo interstate branching for domestic and non-US banks. It has the power to authorize interest-bearing commercial checking accounts.

New concentration limits for mergers and acquisitions involving depository institutions are set by this title. Tighter lending limits and restrictions on the affiliate transactions are also provided. The regulations of the grandfathered unitary thrift holding companies also are changed, and the framework for supervision and examination of bank and thrift holding companies and nonbank subsidiaries are enhanced.

Volcker Rule

This rule bans banking entities from engaging in proprietary trading, acquisition of equity, partnership or ownership interest, or the provision of hedge fund or private equity fund. Systemic nonbank financial companies that are not covered by the Volcker Rule require the FRB to add additional capital requirements and quantitative limits on proprietary trading, investments, and private fund activities.

The Volcker Rule affects banking entities. These entities include insured depository institutions, companies that control an insured depository institution, companies that are treated as a bank holding company under the Bank Holding Company Act, and any subsidiary and affiliates to the banking entities.

Nonbank financial banks are not primarily subjected to the restrictions posed by the Volcker Rule. These companies that are engaged in financial activities have to be designated as systemic by the FSOC and will be subject to additional capital requirements and qualitative limits.

While the Volcker Rule bans proprietary trading, it does not impose its restrictions on commodities such as precious or base metal, agriculture or energy products, and foreign exchanges and loans. Covered instruments held for investment are not covered by the ban. Exemptions to the Volcker Rule apply to proprietary trading. There are some general exemptions. Insurance companies and offshore trading activities are also exempted under certain conditions.

A ban is set on certain relationships with hedge funds and private equity funds. The Volcker Rule generally prohibits a banking entity from investing or sponsoring a covered fund and entering into transactions that could be a covered transaction. The Volcker Rule gives the FRB the authority to implement a limited exemption to covered transaction for prime brokerage transactions.

These bans can be exempted under certain circumstances. The de minimis exemption permits a banking entity to invest in covered funds organized and offered by banking entities for establishing a fund so that it can attract unaffiliated investors and for making a de minimis investment. The fiduciary exemption allows a banking entity to organize and offer a covered fund.

There are offshore exemptions to relationships with covered funds also. These are similar to those offshore exemptions of proprietary trading. Banking entities are given permission to make investments in small business investment companies that are devoted to promote public welfare.

The FSOC requires that banking entities study and make recommendations of the provision of the Volcker Rule within six months of the date of the Dodd-Frank Act's enactment. Federal banking agencies, the SEC, and the CFTC are to consider the study's findings and adopt rules to carry out Volcker Rule requirements. The Volcker Rule should be enacted in the first 12 months from the date where the final rules are issued.

Other Provisions

This title prohibits placement agents, initial purchasers, underwriters, and sponsors of an asset-backed or synthetic asset-backed security from engaging in any transaction that would involve or result in any "material conflict of interest" with respect to any investor in the security. It prohibits the FDIC from approving any application for deposit insurance filed after November 23, 2009. It provides limited exceptions for failing institutions, mergers or acquisitions at the parent commercial firm level, and acquisitions of less than 25% of publicly traded companies.

The OCC and the FDIC are authorized to approve applications for de novo interstate branches of national banks and state nonmember banks, if a state bank chartered by the state where the branch is located is permitted to establish the branch. The Federal Reserve Act (FRA), the HOLA, and the FDIA can eliminate prohibitions against payment of demand deposit interests, thus authorizing the interest-bearing commercial checking accounts.

The Dodd-Frank Act imposes concentration limits on financial companies. The Act implies that the FRB should examine the bank and thrift holding companies and their subsidiaries. It insists that the FRB also regulates nonbank subsidiaries and details additional restrictions on the financial holding companies. Interstate bank acquisitions get a more enhanced set of standards and regulations.

Derivatives, repos (repurchase agreements), reverse repos, and securities have their lending limits. The Dodd-Frank Act prohibits asset purchases from insiders and asset sales to insiders. The FRA has to expand the reach of the affiliate transaction restrictions. The Act prohibits the conversion of troubled institutions. Conversion is permitted if a plan is developed by the new regulator.

The FRB should demand that any financial activity conducted by the grandfathered unitary thrift holding company should be conducted through a newly established intermediate holding company that will subject the FRB regulation as the thrift holding company. The FRB must be ready with regulations to deal with such new thrift holding companies.

The Dodd-Frank Act eliminates the statutory elective investment bank holding company framework that was monitored but recently abandoned by the SEC. It is replaced by a new framework for the supervision of securities holding companies. These companies own or control one or more SEC registered brokers-dealers.

The Act requires federal banking agencies to study the bank investment activities within 18 months of its enactment. The FRB should issue regulations to bank holding companies regarding the capital requirements. Additional restrictions are laid on any thrift that fails to become or remain qualified as thrift lender to pay dividends.

Title VII: Wall Street Transparency and Accountability

This title establishes regulatory frameworks for over-the-counter and security-based swap markets. It imposes exchange trading for derivative contracts. Along with exchange trading, it also imposes new capital, margin requirements, and reporting obligations on over-the-counter swap dealers and major over-the-counter swap participants. Swap dealers and swap participants would be required to clear swaps through a clearinghouse and would execute their transactions on a centralized exchange.

This title levels the playing field for community banks by prohibiting the Federal Reserve or the FDIC from assisting depository institutions involved in swap markets with certain exceptions.

Swaps

Any agreement, contract, or transaction that is an option for the purchase or sale, or is based on the value, of an underlying financial or economic interest or property, or that provides for any purchase, sale, payment, or delivery that is dependent on the occurrence, nonoccurrence, or the extent of the occurrence, of an event associated with a potential financial, economic, or commercial consequence, is called a swap.

A security-based swap is any agreement, contract, or transaction that is a swap and is based on a narrow-based security index, a single security or loan, or the occurrence, nonoccurrence, or the extent of the occurrence of an event relating to a single issuer of a security or the issuers of securities in a narrow-based security index, provided that such event directly affects the financial statements, financial condition, or financial obligations of the issuer.

Mixed swaps are security-based swaps that are based on the value of one or more financial or economic interests or property, or the occurrence, nonoccurrence, or the extent of the occurrence of any event or contingency associated with a potential financial, economic, or commercial consequence.

A swap entity is any swap dealer, security-based swap dealer, major swap participant, or major security-based swap participant. A swap entity may be provided with federal assistance. U.S. banks, U.S. branches, and foreign banks are eligible for federal assistance. Banking institutions that are required to register themselves as swap entities for their swap activities would not receive federal assistance.

The use of advances from any Federal Reserve credit facility or discount window or FDIC insurance or guarantee is termed "federal assistance." Banks would be expected to push out all derivative activities such as hedging, market making, and other intermediary activities to separate them from nonbanking institutions that do not receive federal assistance. The depository institutions are required to push out activities that are based on reference assets that banks may not invest in, most commodities, equity securities, and uncleared credit default swaps (unless they enter into hedging activities).

Swap Regulations

The CFTC and the SEC should consult with each other and then develop regulations for swaps, swap dealers, swap participants, and swap entities. The FSOC resolves any disputes between the SEC and CFTC. The swap participants are expected to adhere to reporting, recordkeeping rules, clearing and execution requirements, and capital and margin rules.

Although the CFTC has jurisdiction over swaps, swap dealers, and major swap participants, the SEC will have jurisdiction over security-based swaps, security-based swap dealers, and major security-based swap participants. A swap can be cleared only after its engagement of a submission for clearing. The applicable agency will go through every swap or group, type, class, or category of swap to determine whether the swap can be cleared.

The clearinghouse also submits the swaps it would be clearing to the applicable agency. The agency will review whether the submission is consistent with the clearing agency's requirements. The clearing requirements are not applicable to the swap if it is not a financial company.

All swaps that are subjected to clearing requirements must be traded on swap execution facility. This facility is a trading system or platform in which more than one participant has the ability to trade swaps by accepting bids made by other participants. The execution requirement does not become applicable until the available swaps are traded by the swap execution facility.

The swap dealer or the swap participant must be registered with the applicable agency. If a swap wants to register with the CFTC, then the swap has to apply to the CFTC, irrespective of it being registered with the SEC.

Each swap dealer or swap participant is required to maintain a perfect audit trail to conduct accurate trade reconstructions, and is required to disclose data regarding transactions, such as price and volume.

Federal banking regulators and the applicable agency for swap dealers and participants set the minimum capital requirements and the minimum initial and variation margin requirements. The CFTC and SEC consult each other for the minimum and maximum requirements and extent possible.

Swap-Facilitating Organizations

A facility cannot trade or process swaps unless it is registered as a swap execution facility. To register itself as a swap execution facility, the facility will have to comply with certain requirements. The depository institution that is registered with the SEC is also registered with the CFTC as the derivatives clearing organization. These derivatives clearing organizations acted as the clearing agencies for swaps before the enactment of the Dodd-Frank Act. To register themselves, the derivatives clearing organizations will also have to adhere to the mandatory requirements.

A swap data repository is any person that collects and maintains information or records based on transactions or positions in, or the terms and conditions of, swaps entered into by third parties for the purpose of providing a centralized record-keeping facility for swaps. Each swap should report to a registered swap data repository. The repository must also comply with certain requirements.

Security-Based Swap Markets

Security-based swaps are considered to be securities for the purposes of the Securities Exchange Act of 1934. When a security-based swap is bought or sold, the concept of beneficial ownership of securities comes into play. The beneficial ownership provision in the act is amended. A person can acquire the beneficial ownership of an equity security based on the purchase or sale of a security-based swap.

Security-based swaps are considered to be securities for the purposes of the Securities Act of 1933. Unless a registration statement is in effect for a security-based swap, no person can offer to sell or buy a security-based swap from or to any person who is not an eligible contract participant. The Investment Advisers Act of 1940 and the Investment Company Act of 1940 are not changed. Even their definitions of securities remain the same.

Title VIII: Payment, Clearing, and Settlement Supervision

This title allows systemic approach for certain financial market payments, payment, clearing, and settlement systems. It establishes uniform risk management standards for systemically significant payment, clearing, and settlement activities. The standards are applicable even to institutions that operate systems in which the above-mentioned activities are carried out.

A financial marketing utility (FMU) is an entity that manages a multilateral system for clearing, transferring, or settling payments, securities, or other financial transactions. Under Title VIII, a broad range of fund transfers, securities, and commodity contracts, swaps, repurchase agreements, derivatives contracts, and any similar transactions that are determined by the Financial Stability Oversight Council are financial transactions.

The Federal Reserve Board and other federal regulators are involved in designating the FMU systemically significant. The FSOC can waive or modify the normal designation process with the emergency powers it is vested with, if it thinks it the right way to mitigate the threats to financial stability. Federal regulators can prescribe risk management standards to the FMU. The title does not allow the FSOC or FRB to make swap or securities-based swap clearing determination that are within SEC's or CFTC's authority.

Under this title, the FMU receives modest financial benefits. FMUs that want to make changes to their rules, procedures, or operations that could materially affect the nature of risks presented by the FMUs will have to follow an advance notice process.

The enforcement of FMUs and their supervision are vested with the federal supervisory agencies. But each supervisor will have to supervise the FMUs annually to determine their operation and perceived risks irrespective of the nature of the risks. The FRB is authorized to appeal to the supervisory agency to enforce actions in an FMU. The FRB may also take enforcement actions against the FMU at times of emergency. But this can be done only after the FRB's consults with FMU's primary supervisor and a majority vote from the FSOC.

In addition to the regular supervision done by the primary federal supervisory agency, financial institutions will have to face a separate examination by the federal supervisory agency with reference to the activities they carry out (mentioned in Section 805 of the Dodd-Frank Act).

There are provisions under which the federal supervisory agencies and the FSOC can share information regarding the designated FMU. The FSOC has the authority to require information from any FMU under reasonable cause, to assess whether the FMU is systemic or not.

Title IX: Investor Protections and Improvements to the Regulation of Securities

This title protects investors in securities. Under this title, the SEC has the authority to hold brokers and dealers who provide investment advice to the same standards to which investment advisers are held. The title establishes the Office of Credit Ratings within the SEC, and this office protects the ratings from being influenced by conflicts of interests.

The SEC is required to conduct a study of whether the establishment of the fiduciary duty standard is necessary. This title requires certain firms to retain ownership interest. The firms deal with package loans and securities and sell them in units. This title introduces many new changes to corporate governance procedures. The title mandates new executive compensation requirements. It also makes it compulsory that advisers of municipalities be registered.

Protecting the Investors

The SEC should conduct a six-month study to determine whether a fiduciary duty standard has to be imposed on broker-dealers who provide personal investment advice to retail customers. The SEC considers the effectiveness of existing standards, gaps between those standards, and standards that are applicable to investment standards. The SEC submits its report to the SBC and the HFSC. At the end of the study, the SEC can develop new rules to close the gaps and remedy overlaps.

The SEC will establish an Investor Advisory Committee. The committee advises the SEC on setting up its priorities for regulation and the substance it can propose, and guides the SEC to promote investor confidence and market stability. Some provisions enhance the SEC by making changes to its management and organizational approach.

The Committee will not be self-funded but will be permitted to maintain a reserve fund from its revenues. This is separate from the amount allocated by the federal budget. The Committee will enjoy a sizable budget in the first five years after the enactment of the Dodd-Frank Act, and it will use a modified budget request approach in the future to Congress. The president and the Office of Management and Budget will also get an additional copy of the request.

The SEC is required to hire a consultant to study its operations and to provide advice on the reforms that the agency will need. After getting the consultant's report, the SEC must submit a report to the HFSC and SBC, at a date no later than six months out. The Comptroller General of the United States must study the employees leaving the SEC for employment in regulated firms within the securities industry. The Comptroller General should also make a report to the HFSC and the SBC within one year. The SEC must annually report the effectiveness of its internal supervisory controls to the HFSC and the SBC.

Federal Securities Law

The antifraud provisions of the federal securities law are extended to apply freely within the United States. The SEC must issue rules to increase the transparency of information available regarding securities lending.

Potential consequences of authorizing a private right of action against any person who aids another person to violate the federal securities laws should be reported to Congress by the GAO.

Credit Rating Agencies and Regulations

In light of the financial crisis, it is clear that the ratings on the financial structured products are inaccurate and uninformative to the investors. The Dodd-Frank Act develops many measures to improve the reliability of the ratings and the operations of those agencies that issue the ratings. The title provides the SEC with greater enforcement tools.

Securitization Process

The Dodd-Frank Act amends the Securities Exchange Act to define asset-backed security, securitizer, and originator. It explains the concept of customary securitization. The Act assigns certain regulators to regulate the various aspects of asset backed securitization. The Dodd-Frank Act, the SEC, the FRB, the FDIC, and the OCC jointly issue rules to retain at least 5% of the credit risk in any asset that the securitizer conveys to a third party by issuing, transferring, and selling an asset-backed security.

The findings of the third-party due diligence report must be disclosed by the issuer or underwriter of the asset-backed security. The SEC must compel the Nationally Recognized Statistical Rating Organization to include a description of representatives, warranties, and enforcement procedures available to investors. These details must be included in any report that accompanies a credit rating.

Corporate Governance

This title of the Dodd-Frank Act provides better insight to shareholders of publicly held companies. The provisions are either extensions or clarifications of existing rules of National Securities Exchange. The title provides guidance on matters pertaining to executive compensation. The SEC need not compel the public companies to include proxy solicitation nominees for directors by the shareholders in their report. But it is necessary for the SEC to pass a requirement insisting that public companies be transparent regarding their appointment of a chairman or a chief executive officer for the second term in office.

Other Changes

There are a number of provisions to change the municipal securities business regulations. The Dodd-Frank Act also changes the operations and role of Public Company Accounting Oversight Board (PCAOB). The PCAOB is allowed to disclose critical information non-U.S. auditor oversight authorities and can review the auditors of brokers-dealers. After review, the information can be issued to the self-regulatory organizations of brokers-dealers.

Title X: Bureau of Consumer Financial Protection

Title X of the Dodd-Frank Act alters the way in which consumer credit is treated. It establishes the Bureau of the Consumer Financial Protection (BCFP). The BCFP is an independent agency that functions to act as a source of funding. The title develops the federal regulation of disclosure and the state law of fairness and suitability. The BCFP has the power to prohibit unfair practices. It oversees the mortgage reform and sees to the enforcement of Title XVI of the Dodd-Frank Act.

Bureau of Consumer Financial Protection

This office is a federal independent agency. The Dodd-Frank Act places the once-abandoned BCFP within the FRB. The director of BCFP is appointed for a term of five years and will have to be a member of the

FSOC and the FDIC's board of directors. The FRB is prohibited by the Act from intervening in the appointment or removal of any director or employee in the BCFP. The FRB does not have the authority to consolidate or merge the BCFP either.

The BCFP concentrates primarily on the areas of research, community affairs, and tracking and collection of complaints. Four offices come under the supervision of the BCFP:

1. Office of Fair Lending and Equal Opportunity
2. Office of Financial Education
3. Office of Service Member Affairs
4. Office of Financial Protection for Older Americans

The BCFP should provide timely assistance to borrowers of educational loans. The Consumer Advisory Board established within the BCFP offers expert services in the areas of consumer protection, financial services, community development, fair lending, and consumer financial practices or services.

Initially, the BCFP is funded by the FRB's budget. The BCFP will receive 10% of the FRB's total operating costs for the fiscal year 2011, 11% for fiscal year 2012, and 12% for the fiscal year 2013 and beyond to avoid unnecessary conflicts. If allocations are insufficient, the BCFP's director will have to submit a written proposal to the president and the Appropriations Committee of the House and Senate.

The BCFP takes enforcement action against any person who engages in the provision of a financial product or service to a consumer. Along with supervision, the BCFP may impose registration requirements on nondepository institutions. The BCFP has the authority to supervise, examine, and enforce action against banks, thrifts, and credit unions. The BCFP is also authorized to regulate service providers. The BCFP is exempted to act for certain persons or activities.

Numerous consumer laws, unfair, deceptive or abusive acts or practices, and mortgage lending require the BCFP to make rules to regulate them. The BCFP will increase the presence of more stringent laws and also increase the compliance burden on lenders. Congress designates the BCFP to coordinate with the SEC, the CFTC, the Federal Trade Commission, and other federal and state regulators. By doing so, the BCFP can consistently regulate consumer financial products and services.

The BCFP will have to coordinate its supervisory functions with the federal prudential regulators and state banking authorities for nondepository institutions. The federal banking agencies are granted permission to access any report of examination or financial condition prepared by the BCFP. The ability of national banks and federal thrifts to rely on federal preemption of state consumer laws is reduced by the Dodd-Frank Act. Along with preemption, the ability of national banks and federal thrifts to operate subsidiaries is also taken away. The lack of preemption will affect the national banks and federal thrifts when it comes to offering uniform financial products nationwide.

The authority of a state attorney general to subpoena a national bank or federal thrift to a court in connection with preempted state laws is restricted by the Act. The BCFP has broader enforcement powers. Upon the receipt of a notice from the state attorney general, the BCFP can intervene and take action against any covered person and enforce provisions of this title.

The amendment to the Dodd-Frank Act, proposed by Senator Richard Durbin, aims to lower the consumer transaction costs related to purchases made with debit cards. The FRB determines whether the debit interchangeable fee is reasonable and makes adjustments to reduce costs incurred by issuers while preventing frauds in debit transactions.

The BCFP must conduct a study on consumers' mandatory predispute arbitration privileges, and consumers' access to information and report them to Congress. The Truth in Lending Act covers consumer credit transactions in an amount up to $50,000 after the Dodd-Frank Act. The Equal Credit Opportunity Act is amended to expand its functionality in collecting information on small businesses. The Electronic Funds Transfer Act is amended to cover remittance transfers.

The secretary of Education must report to Congress on private educational loans and private educational lenders. The report should cover data regarding the growth and changes in the private education market. The secretary must make recommendations to end the conservatorship of Fannie Mae and Freddie Mac and report them to Congress.

The policy statements and sentencing guidelines applicable to frauds and fraud offenses pertaining to the financial institutions should be reviewed.

The Dodd-Frank Act has compensation, seniority, and benefits and employment-related provisions for the transfer of certain functions, authority, and personnel from federal regulatory agencies, the FTC, Department of Housing and Urban Development, and other federal agencies. The designated transfer date cannot be earlier than 6 months or later than 12 months. The effective dates correspond to the designated transfer date.

Title XI: Federal Reserve System Provisions

The FRB's ability to provide financial assistance in the future is restricted by the Dodd-Frank Act. The title gives authority to the GAO to conduct a one-time audit of Federal Reserve emergency lending during times of financial crisis. The FRB has to establish policies and procedures to govern the emergency lending authority.

The FRB ensures that the emergency lending program does not aid failing financial companies, and it protects the taxpayers from losses. The GAO also audits the FRB. The FRB is required to report all the financial assistance information it has provided from December 1, 2007, to July 21, 2010. The FDIC has the authority to guarantee debts of banks and bank holding companies.

Title's Provisions

The FRB is given the authorization to lend financial assistance to financial companies by the FRA. But the FRB's authority to lend financial assistance is limited. The FRB can establish regulations only in consultation with the Treasury. If a loan or any other assistance under Section 13(3) to a financial company is outstanding, and the financial company is subjected to orderly resolution, then the net loss realized by the FRB is given the same treatment as that of a claim raised by the Treasury in a U.S. Bankruptcy Code.

The FDIC's authority to provide general liquidity to insured depository institutions in times of financial crunch is reviewed. The FRB and FDIC determine the liquidity event. Then the FDIC must develop programs to guarantee the obligations of solvent insured depository institutions or solvent depository institution holding companies apart from providing any form of equity. The FDIC is prohibited from borrowing funds from the Deposit Insurance Fund established under the FDIA.

In case of default, Title XI considers whether the orderly liquidation process (Title II) should be incorporated before filing a voluntary or involuntary petition to the U.S. Bankruptcy Code.

The GAO is directed to conduct an audit within one year of the enactment of the Dodd-Frank Act. The GAO can audit any Federal Reserve System, open market transaction, discount window loan, or advance through online examinations. Through this examination, the GAO is required to assess the covered transaction's integrity, effectiveness of its securities, collateral policies, and so forth.

The GAO is required to report on its audits and assessments. The public can access the information from an authentic audit web link posted in the home page of the FRB. The GAO would conduct a one-time audit on all the Sections of 13(3) facilities provided from December 1, 2007, to July 21, 2010. The GAO is authorized to assess the facilities' operational integrity, effectiveness of securities and collateral policies, and many more. The assessment made by the GAO should be reported to Congress within one year of Dodd–Frank Act's enactment.

The GAO can also conduct an audit on the governance process of the FRB. It can analyze the diversity in the representation of the conflicts of interest. The result of this examination should be reported to the House and Senate. The permission granted to the GAO to conduct a full audit on the FRB was opposed by Representatives in the House and the FRB, as it was considered an infringement of FRB's independence.

Under this section of the Act, three changes are made to the governance and supervision policy of the Federal Reserve System. The president of the FRB will be elected by the Class B and Class C directors of the bank. The vice chairman for supervision is responsible for making recommendations regarding supervision and regulation of FRB-supervised banks, holding companies, and systemically significant nonbanks.

These changes enhance the independence of the FRB and consolidate the profile, authority, and control of bank supervision. These changes could possibly have prohibited past or present banking officials from serving as the directors of the FRB.

Title XII: Improving Access to Mainstream Financial Institutions

This title increases access to mainstream financial institutions. It provides alternatives to payday loans, and it encourages low- and moderate-income individuals to explore alternatives. These individuals can then create accounts in insured depository institutions. This title has provisions to create programs to provide low-cost loans of $2,500 or less.

The secretary is authorized to establish multiyear programs to assist low- and moderate-level income individuals, minorities, and undeserved families to acquire low-cost access products and services. The secretary also has the authority to establish regulations that will be necessary to implement this title's requirements and can also administer the funds appropriated to programs established under this title.

The secretary aims to enable low- and moderate-level income individuals to establish accounts at federally insured depository institutions that are appropriate to the financial needs of the individuals and also provide low-cost, small loans to low- and moderate-income consumers as an alternative to high-cost "small-dollar loans," such as payday loans.

To mitigate losses, the title amends the Community Development Banking and Financial Institutions Act of 1994 and creates a loan loss reserve fund.

Title XIII: Pay It Back Act

Title XIII is a technical section of the Act and deals with earlier programs for emergency assistance to insured financial institutions. It decreases the Troubled Asset Relief Program (TARP) funds authorized by the Emergency Economic Stabilization Act of 2008. The Act provides that no authority under the Emergency Economic Stabilization Act (EESA) may be used to incur any obligations under any new programs.

This title contains many changes to existing programs that reduce deficit. The amount authorized by TARP is reduced from $700 billion to $475 billion, and the Treasury is prohibited from initiating any new programs under TARP.

The Treasury is required to report to Congress about the sum it receives from the sale of troubled assets purchased, pursuant to EESA. Title XIII requires certain funds from the sale of troubled assets to be used for deficit reduction, and not as offsets for other expenditure raises or revenue reductions.

The director of the Federal Housing Finance Agency is required to submit a report to Congress its plans to support and maintain the U.S. housing industry. At the same time, it has to guarantee the taxpayers that they will not suffer unnecessary losses.

Title XIV: Mortgage Reform and Anti-Predatory Lending Act

This title imposes requirements on mortgage lenders. It prohibits certain financial incentives that would cause a mortgage lender to steer a consumer to a mortgage of higher cost. It also prohibits residential loans unless the customer's ability to repay the loan determined is reasonable. These regulations apply both to mortgage lenders and to depository institutions.

The title creates mortgage originator duty of care, underwriting requirements that depend on the customer's ability to repay a loan at the time of loan origination, and document requirements intended to avoid loans without documentation. It also prohibits steering incentives for mortgage originators, yield spread premiums, and prepayment penalties.

Mortgage Loans

The Mortgage Act has certain origination standards that have to be applied by mortgage lenders in the underwriting for residential mortgage loans. Each mortgage originator must be registered as a mortgage loan originator, according to state and federal laws. Each should utilize the unique identification number provided by the Nationwide Mortgage Licensing System and Registry on all loan documents.

According to the terms of the loan, mortgage originators should never receive any direct or indirect compensation. Mortgage originators are also prohibited from receiving compensation from any person other than the customer. But the provision does not prohibit any person other than the customer from paying the origination fee if the consumer fails to pay the compensation. The mortgage requires a number of provisions issued under the Truth in Lending Act (TILA) by the Bureau of Consumer Financial Protection.

Every creditor must determine whether a customer has a reasonable ability to repay the loan before making the mortgage. The determination must be based on credit history, income, expected income, employment status, and other financial resources.

Creditors who violate the anti-steering provision or ability to repay loan provisions are liable to pay the compensation fee intended to be made by the borrower. The creditors may also have to make the actual and statutory damage payments. Mortgage originators who violate the requirements are liable to pay three times the amount of the compensation received and the cost incurred by the consumer while taking the necessary action, and a reasonable amount as attorney's fees.

The period to claim a violation is increased from one to three years from the date of occurrence. Right now, only state attorneys general are capable of enforcing actions against the violations. Creditors and assignees are not liable to borrowers or coborrowers if borrowers are convicted of acquiring the mortgage loan through fraudulent practices.

The term "high-cost mortgage" is applicable to a broad range of loans. The reference interest rate, points, and fee triggers are lowered for such mortgages. A third trigger, prepayment penalty, is included. Standards pertaining to prepayment penalties and balloon payments are strengthened for protection. A creditor is not required to pay for the violation made if the error is found within 30 days of closing. A similar correction process is permitted if the violation is discovered within 60 days and is unintentional.

The office of housing counseling is established by the Mortgage Act within the Department of Housing and Urban Development (HUD). The office's primary function is to develop and expand home ownership and rental housing counseling. Next it will have to advertise the availability of these services through public service multimedia awareness campaign. The office will be headed by a director appointed by the secretary of the HUD.

A creditor should never make a mortgage loan without first obtaining a handwritten appraisal from a licensed or certified appraiser after the inspection of the property interior by the appraiser and a second appraisal if the property was purchased within 180 days. This is applicable to higher-risk mortgage loans. The GAO is required to conduct a study based on various appraisal matters. Appraisal independence violation is prohibited by the provisions under TILA. The Mortgage Act allocates funds for emergency mortgage relief and neighboring stabilization programs. The regulations of the Mortgage Act must be implemented within 18 months.

Title XV: Miscellaneous Provisions

This title imposes miscellaneous requirements codes and contains a number of provisions that have very little to do with the credit crisis. It is special interest legislation. This title restricts the United States from lending to certain countries that are heavily indebted. Among other provisions, the GAO is required to assess the relative independence, effectiveness, and expertise of inspectors general appointed by the president and has to report the findings.

This title addresses issues unrelated to financial reforms, such as transparency and foreign corruption in underdeveloped countries with large extractive industries, restrictions on the use of U.S. funds by the International Monetary Fund, and industrial use of minerals that originate from the conflicted areas, especially the Democratic Republic of the Congo.

This title specifies the disclosure requirements for companies that operate mines, and any mining company that has gone public must make an annual report stating all payments made to foreign governments or the federal government for development of oil, natural gas, or minerals.

Within one year of the enactment of the Dodd-Frank Act, the FDIC must submit a report to the HFSC and the SBC on its findings about the impact of the distinctions between the core deposits and brokered deposits.

Title XVI: Section 1256 Contracts

This title amends Section 1256 of the Internal Revenue Code. Section 1256 does not apply to certain derivative contracts transacted on exchanges. It is not required for any interest rate swap, currency swap, basis swap, interest rate cap, interest rate floor, commodity swap, equity swap, equity index swap, credit default swap, or similar agreement to be "marked to market."

The resulting gain or loss from such sale is favorably treated as 60% long-term capital gain or loss and 40% short-term capital gain or loss. Title XVI excludes certain swap transactions from this preferential treatment, including (i) interest rate swaps, currency swaps, commodity swaps, equity swaps, equity index swaps, credit default swaps, and similar agreements; and (ii) securities future contracts or options thereon unless the contract or option is a dealer securities future contract. The provisions of Title XVI will apply to taxable years following enactment of this Act.

Summary

- The Financial Stability Oversight Council, comprised of ten voting members and five nonvoting members, monitors the financial system to pinpoint factors that would cause systemic risk.

- The Office of Financial Research collects, analyzes, and shares data to monitor and measure risks.

- Insurance companies and nonbank financial companies that are excluded from the Federal Deposit Insurance Corporation and Securities Investor Protection Corporation may be liquidated in an orderly fashion, and taxpayer funds may not be used to prevent liquidation.

- The Office of Thrift Supervision will be dismantled and its powers distributed among the Office of Comptroller of the Currency, Federal Deposit Insurance Corporation, and Board of Corporations.

- The Private Fund Investment Advisers Registration Act requires registration and reporting by previously exempted private advisers, with limited exemptions to foreign private advisers, private fund advisers, and venture capital fund advisers.

- The Federal Insurance Office will collect information, monitor the insurance industry, and provide recommendations to modernize insurance regulations; it does not apply to health insurance, long-term care insurance, and crop insurance.

- The Volcker Rule restricts certain bank and bank-related companies from engaging in proprietary trading, hedge fund investing, and private equity fund investing that amounts to more than 3% of Tier I capital.

- The Commodity Futures Trading Commission and the Securities and Exchange Commission will develop regulations for over-the-counter and security-based swap markets.

- Uniform risk management standards have been established for systemically significant payment, clearing, and settlement activities.

- Investors will be better protected by the Office of Credit Ratings, which will prevent conflicts of interest from influencing ratings agencies, and the SEC, which will hold brokers and dealers who provide investment advice to the same standards as investment advisers.

- The Bureau of Consumer Financial Protection encompasses the Office of Fair Lending and Equal Opportunity, the Office of Financial Education, the Office of Service Member Affairs, and the Office of Financial Protection for Older Americans.

- The Federal Reserve Board's emergency lending during times of financial crisis is restricted.

- Low- and moderate-income consumers will have greater access to mainstream financial institutions.

- Troubled Asset Relief Program funding has been decreased, and the U.S. Treasury is prohibited from initiating new programs under TARP.

- A mortgage originator has a duty of care, underwriting requirements pertaining to a consumer's ability to pay, and document requirements.

CHAPTER 4

Institutions Impacted

After reading this chapter, you will be able to:

- Understand the impact of the Dodd-Frank Act on foreign banking organizations.

- Understand the implications of the Act for swap dealers and major swaps participants.

- Grasp the role of the Federal Insurance Organization in overseeing the U.S. and international insurance markets.

- Understand the mortgage banking examination requirements of the Consumer Financial Protection Bureau.

- Comprehend the implications of the dissolution of the Office of Thrift Supervision and the Volcker Rule on banks, thrifts, and bank holding companies.

The Dodd-Frank Act is one of the more complicated regulations that are in place today. Businesses, financial firms, and other organizations have begun to understand the many facets of the Act and the inherent complications. The Act has an impact on several distinct market segments. Enactment of the Act marks the beginning of a new age of financial reform. It shifts the rulemaking efforts to federal agencies, and many people say that the regulators are instrumental in determining the impacts of the Act. Some of the institutions impacted by the Dodd-Frank Act are described in this chapter.

Foreign Banking Organizations

The Dodd-Frank Act has its impacts on foreign bank holding companies and foreign nonbank financial companies. A foreign bank holding company with a consolidated asset value of $50 billion or more is automatically determined to be a systemically significant institution.

Any foreign banking organization (FBO) that meets the size criteria on the basis of consolidation of assets, even the FBO that only has a branch or agency office, is defined[1] as a foreign bank holding company. It is not necessary that the FBO owns a U.S. bank in order to be treated as a foreign bank holding company. But it is not clear whether consolidation of assets will include the FBO's homeland assets or the assets that are based in the United States.

When U.S. assets alone are taken into consideration, the risks that threaten the stability of the U.S. financial system are easier to comprehend. This is easier than looking at risks across the entire global financial system.

A foreign nonfinancial bank is deemed systemically important by the Financial Stability Oversight Council (FSOC) when two-thirds of the Council, including the chairperson (secretary of Treasury), decide that the financial crunch of the foreign nonbank financial company is going to pose a threat to the financial stability of the U.S. financial system. Before a foreign nonbank financial company is determined as systemic, its scope, the scale at which it carries out its activities, and the importance of its operations in the United States should all be considered.

Both the foreign bank holding companies and the foreign nonbank financial companies are subjected to heavy prudential standards when they are determined to be systemically significant institutions. But the Federal Reserve Board (FRB) and the FSOC must clearly differentiate the banking and nonbank financial companies before they apply these prudential standards to the systemic FBOs.

Both FRB and FSOC should maintain a certain amount of discretion when they apply prudential standards to different types of institutions. This principle is applicable to individual institutions also. The standards of the FBOs that are applicable in the home countries are applied to the standards for comparable U.S. bank holding companies.

The rate at which the Basel Banking Committee, G20, and FSOC proceed on their key reforms decides the level of difficulty in assessing comparability in key prudential areas. The FBOs with intermediate U.S. holding companies and systemic nonbank financial companies have to comply with risk-based capital requirements and leverage limits. Compliance with the Volcker Rule will facilitate proprietary trading and sponsoring or investing in hedge funds or private equity funds.

It is not necessary for foreign nonbank financial companies to comply with the Volcker Rule. But they will have to maintain a capital requirement against investments and prohibited activities of bank holding companies.

FBOs that may want to become swap dealers do not enjoy the safe harbor provision of the Dodd-Frank Act to carry out swap activities that will not trigger the FRB and FDIC financial support. If a technical correction bill is passed, then the safe harbor provision will be passed on to FBO branches and agencies. FBOs receive a national treatment on interstate de novo branching.

Derivatives

The assessment of financial and operational implications of being a swap dealer or a major swaps participant (MSP) for specific products is important for pricing, budgeting, and competitive purposes. The benefits are clearer only when the rules are established. The assessment is very important to banking organizations that will be subjected to affiliate transaction rules.

According to the Push Out Rule, insured depository institutions will be permitted to engage in specific derivative activities and affiliate transactions with swap dealers or MSPs. But this is subjected to the affiliate transaction rules, such as collateral requirements, quantitative limits, arm's-length pricing requirements, and so on.

Many practical aspects will benefit from the rulemaking and interpretation process. It is likely that uncertainties will be cleared up. Some of the uncertainties are:

- Margin arrangements on existing or grandfathered trading practices
- Application of portfolio margin requirements on noncleared trades
- Employment of noncash collateral
- Exemption of corporate end users from margin requirements on noncleared trades

As soon as the central clearing mandates become effective, the bilateral trades executed with the help of swap dealers (centrally noncleared or not traded on an exchange) will require posting of initial margins determined by the Commodities Futures Trading Commission (CFTC) and the Securities and Exchange Commission (SEC). With this posting of collateral, the impact of swap entities liquidity may become significant.

Banking organizations that engage in derivatives activities through an insured banking subsidiary should assess the benefits and costs of engaging in such activities. The Dodd-Frank Act may complicate centralized management of risks, affect the ability to centrally manage firm-wide liquidity, optimize multiproduct netting groups, prompt consideration of multiple memberships in clearinghouses to moderate back-to-back trades, and increase the potential for competitive inequality among firms.

The impact of the Dodd-Frank Act on banking organizations and their counterparties shows that banks and derivatives dealers face higher capital requirements and usage of credit limits and lower profitability.

Insurance Companies

The Federal Insurance Organization (FIO) plays a major role in overseeing and coordinating the United States and the international insurance market. The FIO is applicable to all insurance companies except health, crop, and long-term insurance companies. Other provisions of the Dodd-Frank Act are applicable to insurance companies that own broker-dealers, investment advisers, and thrift or banking institutions.

The Act does not define the specific activities of the FIO. The FIO collects information related to insurance industry. It evaluates the potential risks that threaten the insurers in the U.S. and the global market. The FIO has the capacity to enter into information-sharing agreements with other regulatory bodies.

The Dodd-Frank Act has provisions for preemption of state insurance measures. This preemption clause of the Act does not provide the FIO or Treasury the authority to supervise or regulate insurance business.

The Property Casualty Insurers Association of America, through a statement by president and chief executive David A. Sampson, characterized the president's signing of the Dodd-Frank Act as "half time" in the overall financial reform process. "The rule development stage will be just as important for identifying and minimizing overly broad regulation that will result in negative consequences for consumers," Sampson said.[2]

Consumers and Mortgage Banking

The Consumer Financial Protection Bureau (CFPB) regulates and supervises consumer compliance. The CFPB is part of the Federal Reserve System. The CFPB influences the methods of examination and how they are carried out. Firms should be organized according the requirements of the CFPB. Firms may appoint compliance officers to cover each CFPB department.

The CFPB focuses on risk when it carries out its examinations. The frequency at which the examination should be carried out for different firms still has not been specified. Banks and credit unions with a consolidated asset value below $10 billion will be examined by their current regulators. The CFPB has the authority to participate in examinations conducted by other regulators. It can also provide inputs on the content and methods of examination. The CFPB lacks the authority to examine smaller institutions.

The Dodd-Frank Act brings about many changes that have been expected for a long time. The Act favors simple mortgage products and has a changed perspective when it comes to dealing with consumers and mortgage lenders. The provisions supporting origination, inclusion of enhanced monetary damages, new defenses in foreclosure, and additional risk retention requirement are new.

Broker-Dealers

The Dodd-Frank Act has impacted broker-dealers and their registered representatives who provide investment advice and recommendations on securities and who sell mutual funds, variable annuities, and other securities to retail customers.

Broker-dealers should have consistent ways to make decisions and settle terms and sanctions. The enforcement is not dependent on the SEC adopting fiduciary standards for broker-dealers. Most enforcement action involving violations of broker-dealers' suitability requirements are brought by the Financial Industry Regulatory Authority (FINRA). Broker-dealers need additional regulatory measures and governance efforts relating to designations and qualifications.

Banks, Thrifts, and Bank Holding Companies

The Dodd-Frank Act abolished the Office of Thrift Supervision (OTS) and transferred its power to the Office of the Comptroller of Currency (OCC) and the FRB. This helps in the regulation of thrift industry. As OCC and FRB are banking regulators, the convergence of banking and thrift prudential standards happens easily. Under the FRB, savings and loan holding companies are subjected to a greater level of regulatory measures. The regulations were less stringent before the Dodd-Frank Act.

The FRB must take the capital adequacy provisions of the Dodd-Frank Act into consideration when it is involved in the rulemaking process. The Act will require a hike in the capital held by banking firms, bank holding companies, and savings and loan holding companies.

Companies that rely on hybrid capital instruments for capital adequacy requirements will have to depend on readjusted capital structures if they are not grandfathered organizations. Savings and loan holding companies that are exempted from capital adequacy requirements will be subjected to standards that reevaluate their capital adequacy needs.

The Volcker Rule imposes restrictions on the ability of banks, thrifts, and bank holding companies to engage in proprietary trading and sponsor hedge or private equity funds. These restrictions are based on the rule-writing process of the federal banking and securities agencies. Banking companies must closely monitor the rule-writing process. This is necessary to determine the appropriate course of action for rule writing.

Publicly traded companies will have to be compliant and adhere to the provisions of executive compensation. The interagency guidance on executive compensation for financial firms becomes the foundation for these statutory requirements.

The Dodd-Frank Act impacts risk retention requirements, private fund advisers, asset managers, SEC management and enforcement, banks and bank holding companies, large asset managers, and non-U.S. asset managers. The FRB and the Financial Deposit Insurance Corporation (FDIC) will require banks and financial firms to prepare resolution plans for companies to find a safe way to make solvent the financial company in case of failure. For some titles, the Act does not take effect for years. The issues in Fannie Mae and Freddie Mac are still unresolved, and they depend on new lawmaking.

The Dodd-Frank Act promotes a safer system of regulation. The innovations of the Act may shift but not alter the dynamics of the economy. The legislation itself cannot bring greater heavier impacts on the broader economy. The unanticipated consequences of the Act are of concern. After full enactment of the Dodd-Frank Act, not all of its innovations will prove successful.

The major regulatory agencies must work to reshape their institutions. Through this effort they can have lasting impact on financial regulatory reform.

Summary

- The Dodd-Frank Act has an impact on several distinct market segments.

- Foreign banking organizations with a consolidated asset value of $50 billion or more are considered systemically significant under the Act.

- The impact of derivatives-related provisions will not be fully known until related regulations are written and implemented.

- The Act's provisions for insurance companies are broadly written, and related regulations likely will clarify the role of the Federal Insurance Organization.

- The Consumer Financial Protection Bureau lacks the authority to examine banks and credit unions with a consolidated asset value below $10 billion, but can participate in examinations by other regulators.

• The Act increases capital requirements for banking firms, bank holding companies, and savings and loan holding companies.

Notes

1. Dodd-Frank Act–Section 102(a)(1) and (4).
2. www.pciaa.org/LegTrack/web/NAIIPublications.nsf/lookupweb content/4CC8D624CA5836DA86257767004EB2E?opendocument

CHAPTER 5

Dodd-Frank Act Rulemaking

After reading this chapter, you will be able to:

- Know that the Dodd-Frank Act has more than 240 rulemaking provisions.
- Understand that the Securities and Exchange Commission has the authority to design rules to define and fill the gaps in the Act.
- Comprehend the implications of the Act on corporate governance.
- Understand that rules need to be set forth regarding investment advisers, securities lending, arbitration, swaps, credit rating agencies, and securitization.
- Understand that the Act amends or impacts myriad other laws.

The 2,000-page legislation of the Dodd-Frank Act is not an end; it is a beginning. The bill has more than 240 rulemaking provisions, 67 one-time reports or studies, and directs the preparation of an additional 22 periodic reports. The impact of the Dodd-Frank Act will not be known for many years to come. There are 95 provisions in Dodd-Frank concerning

Securities and Exchange Commission (SEC) rule making, followed by U.S. Commodity Futures Trading Commission (CFTC), which has 61.

An integrated risk and compliance framework will limit the wide demarcations between the databases and reporting structures. Consolidation of data into the integrated system will be difficult, but the approach will enable a good start for these regulatory agencies.

SEC and Rulemaking

The Dodd-Frank Act gives the SEC the authority to design rules that will aid in defining and filling the gaps in the legislation. The Act has 95 provisions dealing with the SEC. The SEC is required by the Act to prepare a total of 17 reports. The SEC is second only to the Government Accountability Office (GAO) in the number of reports required to submit. (The GAO has to submit 23 reports.) The SEC's reports will be based on these studies:

- The SEC will have to conduct a study on the state of short selling and the incidence of failure to issue shares sold short and the delivery of shares on the fourth day following the short sale of transaction.

- It should complete a study including public comment on any shortcomings in the conduct's standards and the supervision of broker-dealers and investment advisers.

- It should study the ways to improve the financial literacy of retail investors, effective means of communicating costs, and conflicts of interests in securities investments.

- It should conduct a study to improve investors' access to register information about investment advisers, broker-dealers, and their associated persons.

- The SEC should study ways to enhance examinations for investment advisers and also determine whether the Congress must authorize the SEC to designate self-regulatory organizations (SROs) to help the Commission's examination efforts.

- It should also study the impacts of applying a new test that would extend the reach of the SEC's antifraud provisions.

- The SEC should also study the credit rating process for structured finance products and conflicts of interests connected with issue-payer, subscriber-pay models.

- It should conduct a study on establishing an independent utility to assign the Nationally Recognized Statistical Rating Organization (NRSRO) to determine credit ratings of structured finance products.

- The SEC should complete a study on the independence of NRSRO and its effects on ratings.

- It should study the feasibility and desirability of standardizing credit ratings terminology.

- The SEC should complete the study to reduce the burden of compliance with Sarbanes-Oxley Act (SOX) Section 404(b), which specifies the market capitalization to range between $75 million and $250 million.

The SEC has rulemaking for investment advisers, securities lending, arbitration, swaps, credit rating agencies, securitization, and, most important, corporate governance. Here we look first see the rules related to corporate governance that are created by the SEC. The SEC will play a major role in four regulatory areas:

1. Over-the-counter derivatives
2. Standard of conduct for investment advisers
3. Private fund advisers
4. Credit rating agencies

The SEC will coordinate with prudential regulators that set the capital and margin requirements for bank entities. The SEC has authority over security-based swaps, including credit default swaps. The SEC will retain antifraud jurisdiction over the security-based swap agreements.

The CFTC will share information with SEC that would seal the gap between the two on security-based swap agreements. The SEC has the authority to facilitate provision of simple and clear disclosures to investors. Through adviser registration and reporting, the Dodd-Frank Act will expand to include activities involving hedge funds, private equity funds, and other private investment instruments.

Corporate Governance

Companies will have to disclose whether their employees and directors are allowed to hedge the value of equity securities. All members of the listed companies' compensation committee must be independent within one year of the enactment of the legislation. The compensation committee must consider the independence of the adviser when it selects the consultant, legal counsel, or any other adviser within one year of the enactment of the law.

Companies should disclose the relationship between the executive compensation that is actually paid and the company's financial performance. They should also include whether there are any changes in the value of the companies' shares, dividends, and distributions. The median annual total compensation of all employees except the chief executive officer (CEO), the annual total compensation of the CEO, and the ratio of the median employee annual total compensation to the annual total compensation of the CEO should be disclosed by companies.

Investment Advisers

The rules defining the term "venture capital fund" should be established to exempt investment advisers who solely advise one or more venture capital funds from SEC registration within one year of the Act's enactment. Rules to exempt from SEC registration an investment adviser who acts as an adviser to private funds and has assets under the management of less than $150 million will be developed. Rules must also require each investment adviser to a private fund to file reports with necessary information, and they must also protect the interests of investors or help assess systemic risk.

Securities Lending

Rules should be designed to increase the transparency of information available in regard to the securities lending.

Arbitration

Rules should be developed to prohibit or limit the use of mandatory arbitration predispute agreements between broker-dealers and investment advisers.

Swaps

Rules should be set to report real-time data regarding swap transactions, including price and volume. Rules for business conduct standards for swap dealers and major swap participants must be designed. In addition, rules are to be created for nonbanking institutions regarding capital and uncleared swap margin requirements. Rules should establish limits in connection to hedge exemption provisions and size of positions in any security-based swap. They should require the reporting of uncleared swaps that were entered into before the date of enactment of the Act. Rules should also facilitate the registration of security-based swap dealers and major security swaps participants.

Credit Rating Agencies

Rules should be established to prevent sales and marketing considerations that influence ratings production credit rating agencies. Rules are set to list the procedures and methods used by the credit rating agencies. They should require the credit rating agencies to establish, maintain, and enforce policies that define and disclose the meaning of rating symbols and the application of the rating symbols to all instruments that are used consistently. Rules should ensure that persons employed in the credit rating agencies to perform ratings are tested for knowledge of the rating process; they should also meet standards for training, experience, and competency to produce accurate ratings. In addition, rules for credit rating agencies regarding the current exemption from Regulation FD should be removed.

Securitization

The securitizers of asset-based securities should maintain 5% of the credit risk in assets that are transferred, sold, or conveyed through the issue of asset-based securities. Rules should be set to prohibit against any underwriter, placement agent, initial purchaser, or sponsor of asset-based security from engaging in certain transactions that would result in material conflict of interest. Rules should require issuers of asset-based securities to disclose information pertaining to assets backing each class of security.

Other Legislation

The next sections cover other legislation within the Dodd-Frank Act that is not covered in the previous sections.

Consumer Financial Protection Bureau

The Dodd-Frank Act transfers the authority of Secure and Fair Enforcement for Mortgage Licensing Act (SAFE) to the newly established Consumer Financial Protection Bureau for its efficient administration. The Bureau assumes the responsibility to register with the Nationwide Mortgage Licensing System Registry (NMLS).

The Bureau helps to register individual mortgage loan originator employees who are part of a depository institution, irrespective of its size, and employees of an institution regulated by the Farm Credit Administration.

The new law of SAFE Act has provisions to extend the deadline for NMLS registration system, which is not complete even today. But the NMLS registration system could be completed before the Bureau assumes its responsibility. The SAFE Act also has transferred authority to the Department of Housing and Urban Development (HUD). HUD decides whether the states have implemented a compliant system for the originator employees who were not part of the depository institutions.

HUD has the authority to determine whether states have established a compliant licensing system. In cases where the states have failed to do so, HUD assumes the duty to establish a backup compliant licensing system for the states. After the Dodd-Frank Act is implemented, this responsibility of HUD will be assumed by the Bureau.

The Bureau also assumes additional authority from the SAFE Act. The authority transfer is related to mortgage originator net worth, surety bond, or recovery fund. The Bureau has to create awareness of the regulations established to set up the minimum net worth of mortgage originators or surety bonds requirements for residential mortgage loan originators and minimum requirements for recovery funds that are paid into by loan originators.

Truth in Lending Act

The Dodd-Frank Act amends the Truth in Lending Act and provides a rule to revise the escrow account requirements for high-priced, first-lien, huge mortgage loans. This rule would increase the annual percentage rate (APR) threshold that is used to determine whether a mortgage lender is required to establish an escrow account. Escrow accounts should be established for property taxes and insurances that are first lien in nature, and they also are mandatory for mortgage loans that are huge.

These huge loans are called jumbo loans, and they exceed the conforming loan size limit for the purchase by Freddie Mac as specified by the Dodd-Frank Act. The APR that is established for first-lien loans of the escrow accounts is 1.5% or more; this should be above the applicable prime rate offer.

The escrow requirement is applicable to jumbo loans only if the APR is 2.5% or more above the prime offer rate. But the APR threshold for the nonjumbo loans still remains intact. The Dodd-Frank act revises the regulatory requirement for escrow accounts and the APR threshold. It also establishes provisions for disclosure requirements.

Home Mortgage Disclosure Act

The Dodd-Frank Act addresses the disclosure of information by lenders, and it covers such issues as the age of the borrower, borrower credit score, total points and fees payable at origination, the difference between the loan's interest rate and the treasury note of similar maturity, value of collateral pledged against the loan, and length before loan reset in the new categories amended into the Home Mortgage Disclosure Act (HMDA).

The Act requires 20 new HMDA reporting obligations. These obligation requirements will add compliance costs to every bank function.

Real Estate Settlement Procedures Act

The Dodd-Frank Act amends the Real Estate Settlement Procedures Act (RESPA). It prohibits the service provider of a federally related mortgage loan from obtaining a force-placed insurance. There can be exemptions in cases when the borrower has failed to comply with loan requirements and has decided to maintain hazard insurance. The Act also amends RESPA to prohibit loan providers from charging fees for valid qualified written requests. It requires the loan provider to take timely actions when borrowers request to correct errors pertaining to final loan payoffs or allocation of loan payments.

Electronic Funds Transfer Act

The Electronic Funds Transfer Act (EFTA) is amended to include provisions regarding remittance electronic transfers. The provisions require the remittance transfer providers to disclose the amount of currency that would be received to the senders. The EFTA is further amended to give the Bureau authority in certain areas.

The Bureau can regulate interchange transfer fees of issuers that hold assets with a value greater than $10 billion. This is done to bring down the fees to reasonable levels and make them proportional to the costs incurred by the issuers. The regulation is not applicable to debit cards and generally issued prepaid cards. It can also regulate network fees to ensure that these fees are not used to compensate issuers on electronic debit transfers.

Fair Credit Reporting Act

The Dodd–Frank Act amends the Fair Credit Reporting Act. It requires a lender to provide a consumer with the consumer's numerical credit score and factors that affect the score.

Bank Holding Company Act

The Dodd–Frank Act also amends the Bank Holding Company Act of 1956. It requires bank holding companies and their subsidiaries to provide reports to the federal regulators as part of the supervisory regulation. It allows federal regulators to conduct examinations on the bank holding companies and their subsidiaries. This helps in assessing the financial condition of bank holding companies, identifying risks that threaten the financial stability of the companies and of the United States.

Investment Advisers Act

The Investment Advisers Act of 1940 is amended by the Private Fund Investment Advisers Registration Act under the codes of the Dodd–Frank Act. This amendment alters the landscape for investment advisers to private funds in regulation. Non-U.S. investment advisers who were earlier exempted from registration under the Investment Advisers Act will have to register to comply with the new requirements. But there also are some exemptions when it comes to non-U.S. investment advisers.

Securities Exchange Act

The Dodd-Frank Act amends the Securities Exchange Act of 1934 by the provisions in "Securities Whistleblower Incentives and Protection." The Act keeps intact the enforcement mechanisms of whistleblower protection under the Sarbanes-Oxley Act (SOX). It amends SOX to provide employees with claims a jury trial. SOX also is amended to prohibit the use of predispute arbitration agreements. The agreements, policies, and forms under SOX cannot be waived after this amendment.

The Dodd-Frank Act's amendment clarifies the whistleblower protection provisions. SOX has to clarify whether these provisions are applicable to the employees of subsidiaries of publicly traded companies. Earlier SOX provisions for whistleblower protection were applicable only to employees of publicly traded companies and not to their subsidiaries.

The Dodd-Frank Act gives an employee more time to bring the claim of violations of SOX, and it offers greater remedies. The amendment allows SOX and the Securities Exchange Act to permit existing employees to seek reinstatement and attorney fees and costs as remedies for violations of SOX. While the Securities Exchange Act allows double payback plus interest, SOX allows only payback plus interest.

The amendment made requires aggrieved employees of retaliatory companies to file a complaint with the Occupational Safety and Health Administration within 180 days of the alleged violation of the employee or when the employee is aware of such a violation. The Dodd-Frank Act allows the Securities Exchange Act to permit whistleblowers to bring a court action for the alleged violation within three years after becoming aware of the claim or six years after the violation has occurred.

Summary

- The Dodd-Frank Act is the beginning of financial reform, not the end.

- The Securities and Exchange Commission will play a role in four regulatory areas: over-the-counter derivatives, standard of conduct for investment advisers, private fund advisers, and credit rating agencies.

- Publicly held companies' compensation committees must be independent, and the committees must ensure that advisers are independent.

- The Act includes provisions for disclosing executive compensation in relation to performance metrics.

- The Act amends, enacts, or impacts a host of other laws, including the Secure and Fair Enforcement for Mortgage Licensing Act, the Truth in Lending Act, the Home Mortgage Disclosure Act, the Real Estate Settlement Procedures Act, the Electronic Funds Transfer Act, the Fair Credit Reporting Act, the Bank Holding Company Act, the Investment Advisers Act, and the Securities Exchange Act.

CHAPTER 6

Role of New and Existing Agencies

After reading this chapter, you will be able to:

- Understand the purpose and duties of the Financial Stability Oversight Council.
- Grasp the role of the Office of Financial Research.
- Understand the agencies that fall under the purview of the newly created Bureau of Consumer Financial Protection.
- Understand the regulatory framework for bank holding companies and nonbank financial companies.
- Understand the Dodd–Frank Act's impact on depository institutions.
- Grasp how the Office of Thrift Supervision will be dismantled.
- Understand the expanded roles of the Federal Deposit Insurance Corporation and the Office of Comptroller of the Currency.
- Understand the impact of the Act on the Securities Investor Protection Corporation, Securities and Exchange Commission, Federal Reserve Board, Commodity Futures Trading Commission, and Government Accountability Office.

The Dodd-Frank Act changes the existing regulatory structure by creating a host of new agencies (while merging and removing others) in an effort to streamline the regulatory process, increase oversight of specific institutions regarded as a systemic risk, amend the Federal Reserve Act (FRA), and promote transparency, among additional changes.

The Act: establishes rigorous standards and supervision to protect the economy and American consumers, investors, and businesses; ends taxpayer-funded bailouts of financial institutions; provides for an advanced warning system on the stability of the economy; creates rules on executive compensation and corporate governance; and eliminates the loopholes that led to the economic recession.[1] The new agencies either are granted explicit power over a particular aspect of financial regulation or that power is transferred from an existing agency. All of the new agencies, and some existing ones that are not currently required to do so, are also compelled to report to Congress on an annual (or biannual) basis, to present the results of current plans and to explain future goals.

Important new agencies created include:

- Financial Stability Oversight Council (FSOC)
- Office of Financial Research (OFR)
- Bureau of Consumer Financial Protection (BCFP)
- Office of National Insurance within the Treasury
- Office of Credit Rating Agencies within the Securities and Exchange Commission (SEC)

Title I creates the FSOC and the OFR. The two new offices are attached to the Treasury Department, with the Treasury secretary being chair of the Council and the head of the OFR being a presidential appointment with Senate confirmation.

Financial Stability Oversight Council

The purpose of the FSOC is to:

- Identify risks to U.S. financial stability that may arise from ongoing activities of large, interconnected financial companies and non-financial companies.

- Promote market discipline by eliminating expectations of government bailouts.

- Respond to emerging threats to financial stability.

Some of the duties of the FSOC are to:

- Gather necessary information to access risks to the U.S. financial system.

- Monitor the financial services marketplace and identify potential threats to U.S. financial stability.

- Facilitate information sharing among different regulatory agencies.

- Provide recommendation to the Federal Reserve Board (FRB) on prudential standards.

Meetings are held every quarter at the request of the chairperson.

Any bank or nonbank financial institution with assets above $50 billion has to submit to the FSOC certified reports with the details of financial conditions and risk management system in place.

Office of Financial Research

The Dodd–Frank Act establishes the OFR. The OFR taps data from validated sources. The OFR is empowered to collect, validate, and maintain the tapped data that is necessary to maintain the stability of the U.S. financial system. The OFR has the capacity to analyze the most confidential Wall Street data pertaining to trading and lending.

The OFR requires a periodic submission of reports from member agencies, commercial data providers, data sources that are publicly available, and financial entities to assess the financial market in which the financial activities of financial companies take place.

The Dodd-Frank Act provides the director of the OFR with the power of subpoena. Through this, the director can request the production of particular data. The request is made by the director in a written format, and it is justified only if reason for requisition is to ascertain financial stability status, using the requested data.

Bureau of Consumer Financial Protection

The Dodd-Frank Act creates the BCFP. The BCFP consolidates consumer protection powers of various regulatory agencies. They create regulations and enforce them with a minimum of complications to protect the interests of investors.

According to the Dodd-Frank Act, the BCFP does not have the right to exercise its power and enforce the consumer financial laws over any person who is regulated by the state insurance regulator. The Act establishes the Office of Fair Lending and Equal Opportunity, Office of Financial Education, Office of Service Member Affairs, and Office of Financial Protection for Older Americans under the BCFP.

The impact of the provisions of the Dodd-Frank Act on the BCFP shows that this agency is not intended to regulate the insurance business, although it is fully able to do so when it comes to regulating consumer financial activities.

Bank Holding Companies

The Dodd-Frank Act concentrates on systemic risk concerns. It designates bank holding companies with a consolidated asset value of $50 billion or more as systemically significant institutions. The Act creates two new regulatory bodies for bank holding companies. It also abolishes the Office of Thrift Supervision, the existing body of regulation for the bank holding companies. It also has the authority to deal with the

Federal Deposit Insurance Corporation (FDIC), the FRB, and the Office of the Comptroller of Currency (OCC)—the other three existing regulatory bodies of the bank holding companies.

Bank holding companies investments in hedge and private equity funds are limited. The Dodd-Frank Act establishes a minimum leverage for bank holding companies. Along with this, it also sets up capital requirements based on the risk faced by these bank holding companies.

Nonbank Financial Companies

The Dodd-Frank Act establishes a new regulatory framework for the nonbank financial companies. The Act gives the FSOC the authority to determine which is a systemic nonbank financial company. The Act addresses the lack of an organization's presence to liquidate the assets of nonbank financial companies that are declared systemic.

The Dodd-Frank Act prohibits nonbank financial companies from retaining ownership interest or sponsoring hedge funds or private equity funds when the nonbank financial companies are determined to be systemic. The Act sets up nonbank financial companies' ownership level in a fund to be not more than 3% of the banking entity's own tier 1 capital. Nonbank financial companies that are acknowledged to be systemic are supervised by the FRB at the direction of the Dodd-Frank Act.

Depository Institutions

The Dodd-Frank Act is responsible for setting up capital requirements for depository institutions that are deemed systemic. The federal banking regulators are directed by an amendment in the Act (Collins Amendment) to establish minimum leverage and capital requirements for insured depository institutions.

The Act further mandates that federal banking agencies establish corrective actions specified under the Federal Deposit Insurance Act (FDIA).

Office of Thrift Supervision

The Office of Thrift Supervision (OTS) will be eliminated once the Dodd-Frank Act is enacted. Before elimination, the authority to supervise the federal savings agencies will be transferred to the FDIC. The power to develop new rules for the federal savings agencies is vested with the OCC. But there is also an exemption. The Federal Reserve will acquire the authority to make rules for the affiliate transactions, insider loans, and tying arrangements.

The transfer of authority and power from the OTS to other regulators will have to be done before July 2011, after which the OTS will be eliminated. But an extension of six months is also available in case of any delay in the transfer. The employees of the OTS are also transferred to other federal regulators office upon the elimination of the OTS.

Federal Deposit Insurance Corporation

Under the Dodd-Frank Act, the FDIC regulatory authority is expanded to nonbank financial companies with at least $50 billion in assets. A failed, systemically important nonbank can now be made solvent in a similar manner to that of FDIC-insured depository institutions. The Act also empowers the FDIC to have advance access to information necessary to make solvent a large, complex financial company in an orderly manner.

The Dodd-Frank Act's purpose is to avoid another market meltdown by minimizing moral hazard, mitigating systemic risk, providing for orderly liquidation of nonbank financial companies, and ending "too big to fail." The FDIC has already established a new office of Complex Financial Institutions and Division of Depositor and Consumer Protection (DCP)

The FDIC acts as the deposit insurer and supervises the community banks. The DCP sees to the protection of depositors, depositor compliance examination, and enforcement of depositor requirements.

Office of Comptroller of the Currency

The Dodd-Frank Wall Street Reform and Consumer Protection Act expands the jurisdiction of the OCC by abolishing the OTS and transferring many of its functions to the OCC. The Act also restricts the OCC's preemption power over state law.

One of the effects of the Act is to change the law with respect to operating subsidiaries of national banks. In 2007, the Supreme Court held in *Watters v. Wachovia Bank* that the operating subsidiary of a national bank benefited from the same preemption applicable to its parent. Consequently, the Michigan Office of Insurance and Financial Services could not subject Wachovia Mortgage Corporation to its regulatory requirements.

Also, in the area of consumer protection requirements, the Dodd-Frank Act limits the OCC's ability to preempt state law. In general, in order to preempt state consumer protection laws, the Comptroller needs to find on a case-by-case basis that state law is "inconsistent" with federal law. With this new provision, advantages of a national charter over a state charter have been reduced. Going forward, this may affect the decisions of banks on what type of charter to have.

Orderly Liquidation Authority

The Dodd-Frank Act creates resolution mechanisms for companies whose failure would threaten the stability of the U.S. financial system. The Orderly Liquidation Authority (OLA) comes under the FDIC and is similar to the FDIC's current resolution for insured depository institutions. The OLA creates a federal receivership process.

The OLA replaces the bankruptcy process for systemic companies. The OLA sees to it that the shareholders, creditors, directors, and management bear the losses of the financial company in relation to their responsibilities, such as actions of damages, restitution, and compensation.

The OLA provides the FDIC the authority to address financial companies that are on the brink of financial collapse and helps the FDIC to serve as corporate management, creditor of the corporation, and watchdog of the liquidation process. The Dodd-Frank Act directs the Treasury to establish the Orderly Liquidation Fund. The FDIC will manage this fund.

Securities Investor Protection Corporation

The Securities Investor Protection Corporation (SIPC) was established under the Securities Investor Protection Act of 1970 to protect investors against markets risks and insolvency risks. The Dodd-Frank Act increases the cash sublimit of SIPC from $100,000 to $250,000. The increase in the cash advance amount reduces the difference between the cash and security coverage. The Act ensures the coordination of the Federal Deposit Insurance Corporation and SPIC resolutions, when it comes to dealing with registered broker-dealers.

Securities and Exchange Commission

The Dodd-Frank Act gives the primary implementation authority to the SEC along with other federal agency regulators. The Act provides the SEC with rulemaking authority. With this authority, the SEC is able to limit the arbitration of disputes that are caused as a result of the federal securities laws. The Dodd-Frank Act also provides the SEC with enforcement authority over nonbank securitizers.

While examining regulated firms, the SEC can reject the Freedom of Information Act requests for documents under the Dodd-Frank Act provision. Without this provision, the SEC might have been forced to release documents collected during the examination of credit rating companies and municipal bond advisers.

With the enactment of the Dodd-Frank Act, the SEC passes more authority to the Financial Industry Regulatory Authority to oversee the financial regulations in circulation within the industry. The Act has increased the SEC's funding and has also increased its power to enforce rules and regulations.

Federal Reserve Board

The Dodd-Frank Act transfers the functions of the OTS to the FRB. The FRB takes over the services that are to be rendered to savings and loan holding companies and nondepository institution subsidiaries under the Dodd-Frank Act. The FRB regulates insider loans, affiliate transactions, and tying arrangements.

The FRB must carry out the provisions of the Volcker Rule under the Dodd-Frank Act. It supervises the bank entities and nonbank financial companies while they engage in proprietary trading and hedge fund and private equity fund investment.

The FRB also has to create fraud reduction standards of long-standing nature. The FRB will have to create incentives for issuers, merchants, and networks to comply with them. Under the Act, the FRB has nine months to publicize regulations that will make card interchange fees reasonable.

Commodity Futures Trading Commission

The Commodities Futures Trading Commission (CFTC) has the authority to establish rules to regulate the swaps marketplace. The CFTC implements the Dodd-Frank Act to lower risk, increase transparency, and protect American shareholders. The Act regulates swap dealers by subjecting them to capital and margin requirements. Dealers will have to adhere to specific business conduct standards, and this will promote market integrity by lowering the risks.

The Dodd-Frank Act also requires dealers to meet specific reporting requirements and regulators to do their supervision without hindrance. The Act develops standardized derivatives to encourage open platforms for trading, and these derivatives are submitted to clear central counterparties. Clearinghouses have lowered the risks that threaten the stability of the futures marketplace. The Act will use this fact in the swap marketplace to lower the risks.

The Dodd–Frank Act will have to write rules to regulate the swap marketplace. The CFTC has identified 30 areas[2] where rules are necessary, as shown in the next list.

Comprehensive Regulation of Swap Dealers and Major Swap Participants

   I. Registration

  II. Definitions, such as swap dealer, major swap participant, security-based swap dealer, and major security-based swap participant, to be written jointly with SEC

 III. Business conduct standards with counterparties

 IV. Internal business conduct standards

  V. Capital and margin for nonbanks

 VI. Segregation and bankruptcy for both cleared and uncleared swaps

Clearing

  VII. DCO core principle rulemaking, interpretation, and guidance

VIII. Process for review of swaps for mandatory clearing

  IX. Governance and possible limits on ownership and control

   X. Systemically important DCO rules authorized under Title VIII

  XI. End user exception

Trading

  XII. DCM core principle rulemaking, interpretation, and guidance

 XIII. SEF registration requirements and core principle rulemaking, interpretation, and guidance

 XIV. New registration requirements for foreign boards of trade

  XV. Rule certification and approval procedures (applicable to DCMs, DCOs, SEFs)

Data

 XVI. Swap data repositories registration standards and core principle rulemaking, interpretation, and guidance

 XVII. Data record-keeping and reporting requirements

XVIII. Real-time reporting

Particular Products

XIX. Agricultural swaps

XX. Foreign currency (retail off exchange)

XXI. Joint rules with SEC, such as "swap" and "security-based swap"

XXII. Portfolio margining procedures

Enforcement

XXIII. Antimanipulation

XXIV. Disruptive trading practices

XXV. Whistleblowers

Position Limits

XXVI. Position limits, including large trader reporting, bona fide hedging definition, and aggregate limits

Other Titles

XXVII. Investment adviser reporting

XXVIII. Volcker Rule

XXIX. Reliance on credit ratings

XXX. Fair Credit Reporting Act and disclosure of nonpublic personal information

Government Accountability Office

The Government Accountability Office (GAO) is required to prepare a report on the enactment of the Dodd-Frank Act after conducting a thorough study. The GAO will also study the effects that the legislation has on the availability and affordability of credit for consumers, home buyers, mortgage lending, and small businesses.

The GAO reports on the efforts taken by the government to combat mortgage foreclosure, audits the Federal Reserve facilities, and conducts studies on person-to-person lending and the exemption for smaller issuers. The GAO also studies the securities litigation, nonadmitted insurance market, and self-regulatory organizations for private funds. The GAO reports on accredited investors after a thorough study.

Summary

- In an effort to streamline the regulatory process, the Dodd-Frank Act creates new agencies, merges others, and dismantles others.

- Newly created agencies include the Financial Stability Oversight Council, the Office of Financial Research, the Bureau of Consumer Financial Protection, the Office of National Insurance, and the Office of Credit Rating Agencies.

- The purpose of the Financial Stability Oversight Council is to identify systemic risk, promote market discipline, and respond to emerging threats.

- The Office of Financial Research is empowered to collect, validate, and maintain data, as well as to subpoena data.

- The Bureau of Consumer Financial Protection consolidates many current consumer protection efforts.

- The Office of Thrift Supervision will be dismantled, and bank holding companies will be regulated by the Federal Deposit Insurance Corporation, Federal Reserve Board, and Office of the Comptroller of the Currency.

- The Orderly Liquidation Authority, which is within the Federal Deposit Insurance Corporation, will oversee a federal receivership process for failed companies that pose a systemic economic risk.

- The Securities Investor Protection Corporation will increase the cash sublimit from $100,000 to $250,000.

- The Securities and Exchange Commission has primary implementation authority for the Dodd-Frank Act.

- The Federal Reserve Board will enforce the Volcker Rule.

- The Commodity Futures Trading Commission will regulate the swaps marketplace.

Notes

1. http://banking.senate.gov/public/_files/FinancialReformSummary AsFiled.pdf.
2. Rule Makings, U.S. Commodity Futures Trading Commission, www.cftc.gov/LawRegulation/DoddFrankAct/Rulemakings/index.htm.

CHAPTER 7

Global Impact and Implications

After reading this chapter, you will be able to:

- Understand the ways in which other countries may adopt some provisions of the Dodd-Frank Act.
- Understand the impact of the Act on the U.S. banking industry.
- Understand the implications of the Act for real estate markets and private equity investments.
- Comprehend the impact of the Volcker Rule on large financial institutions.
- Understand the implications of new registration requirements for non–U.S. advisers.
- Grasp how the Act relates to the European debt crisis, Basel III, and the G20.
- Understand how the Act impacts the investment industry.

The Dodd-Frank Act includes a new set of firms in the financial regulatory framework and will regulate new markets by creating new regulators. The Act intends to curb the hazardous effects of the financial crisis and the factors that threaten the financial stability of not only the United States but also other economies of the world.

Banking Industry

The Dodd-Frank Act impacts big banks and the banking industry tremendously. It is said to be very good for the stability of the financial system. The Act also has effects on smaller banks. But the impacts on smaller banks are different from those on bigger banks. It has its effects on capital requirements, returns, leverage, risk taking, transparency, and innovation in both small and large banks.

Some of the aspects of the Dodd-Frank Act can be adopted by other countries as a part of their financial regulatory reform regime. To tackle the financial crisis, the United States has laid out onerous legislation. The rest of the world should follow the United States' speedy development pace and approach to curbing the effects of the financial crunch.

The U.S. banking industry has tight restrictions and limitations on financial activities. But other countries follow a more liberal universal banking model. With a universal banking model, world economies may not be ready to implement the restrictions of the Dodd-Frank Act.

The legislation may be expected to affect the U.S. banking industry in two different ways. The first is that the Act could create a downward pressure on the profitability of the banking industry, and the second is that the Act could create upward pressure on the amount of capital that has to be provided in various forms of business.

When the banking industry and the regulations are correlated, it should be recognized that thus far the banking industry is currently capitalized beyond the demands of the legislations. This is because of the major belief that businesses should be well capitalized.

The financial crisis has shown the need for strong capital requirements. The larger banking companies should have sufficient amounts of capital to sustain the losses that they incur. Systemic problems can be countered successfully only if banking companies have enough capital to enable them in the future to function as financial intermediaries.

To foster this, the Dodd-Frank Act embeds these requirements of the industry into its framework. Every provision in the Act either increases the capital requirements or decreases the profitability.

The Act provides the Consumer Financial Protection Agency with greater authority. Although the agency comes under the Federal Reserve, it has independent authority to carry out its activities. The agency creates a downward pressure on different types of mortgages, lending, and credit card products and a full range of fee-based businesses. The agency also impacts the banking system by affecting profitability.

The provisions for derivatives are complicated. Of the Fortune 500 companies, 150 of the financial companies ended up having derivatives. The treatment that the financial companies received in the Act has been different from that of the nonfinancial companies.

The banking companies have to go through the central clearing system. Under this provision, the liquidity of banking institutions will face higher demands. It is likely that limitations on financial firms engaging in derivatives and investing in private equity funds would not be adopted globally. Along with private equity funds, real estate funds also feel the effect of the Dodd-Frank Act.

Financial reforms made through the Act have a combined effect of impacting debts in real estate and private equity investments in both U.S. and global platforms. It is feared that when the debt capital markets return to their original state, the derisking caused by the financial reforms could lead to slower recovery of real estate debt capital markets. This sentiment is prevalent throughout the world's economies.

The swap push-out provision introduced by Senator Blanche interacts with both nonfinancial companies and financial companies that use derivatives. In spite of strong opposition from the public, the Federal Reserve, the Federal Deposit Insurance Corporation (FDIC), and the White House, this provision has found its place in the Dodd-Frank Act.

As a result of this, banks do not enjoy the high leverage that they enjoyed previously. Most of the banking institutions have deleveraged themselves in the last few years, even to the level of writing themselves down. The decrease in leverage will bring them lower profitability.

Although this provision will support Swap-outs, the banking system tremendously in the provisions in the Collins Amendment that were appended to the Act in its last stages of development specify new capital requirements that are difficult for banks to implement.

Other nations cannot be expected to adopt a concentrated banking system. This could leave them at a disadvantage with the United States, which already has designed elements that are necessary to reform the national financial system. Thus, inconsistency will rise between world economies.

The markets may respond positively to these provisions, but a few problems will have to be dealt with first. The improvement in certainty and derisking is a positive development. These developments have aided the United States in taking a lead in financial reform.

The Volcker Rule blocks the moral hazards and risks that large financial businesses face. It also prevents local banks from growing by merging assets and acquisitions. Bigger banks do not face this restriction because they enjoy the benefits of bailout programs when they face bankruptcy in high-risk investment return situations. If this rule is adopted only in the United States, it probably could weaken the country's financial competitiveness.

But if the rule is implemented globally, it is likely to clash with the rules that govern financial industries of other countries. The merger and acquisition provisions of the Dodd-Frank Act can curb the realization of other countries' dreams to establish megabanks.

Other nations feel that when megabanks continue to participate in high-risk and higher investment returns by following the too-big-to-fail theory, unfair competition and market regulations cannot benefit economies impartially. This could also increase the chances of bigger banks going bankrupt with heavier investments and risks.

The collapse of hedge funds in financial markets could bring inconsistency on an international level. With the implementation of the Act, the Securities and Exchange Commission (SEC) would increase its scrutiny of proprietary strategies of hedge funds and other investments. The United States has an added responsibility of enforcing its domestic financial reform efforts in the international arena.

The Dodd-Frank Act provides exemptions on the registration of investment advisers with the SEC. These exemptions are more restrictive than the one embedded in the current law, the Investment Advisers Act of 1940. The Act requires non–U.S. advisers to private funds who have U.S. investors to register with the SEC and to comply with regulatory requirements applicable to investment advisers registered under the Advisers Act.

Until passage of the Dodd-Frank Act, non–U.S. advisers were exempted from registering with the SEC under these conditions:

- Non–U.S. advisers should have fewer than 15 U.S. clients in the 12 months preceding the registration.

- These advisers should not hold themselves out to the public as investment advisers.

- Non–U.S. advisers should not act as investment advisers to any investment company as defined in the Investment Company Act of 1940.

The exemptions in this provision have permitted non–U.S. advisers to accept subscriptions from U.S. investors for their funds without registering under the SEC. But the restrictions are inflexible.

The new registration requirements specify that:

- Non–U.S. advisers should not have any place of business in the United States.

- They should have a total of fewer than 15 total clients and investors in the United States.

- Their aggregate assets under management (AUM) must be attributed to the clients and investors in the United States.

- The investment advisers should neither hold themselves out to the public as investment advisers nor act as investment advisers to an investment company or business development company.

Currently, non–U.S. advisers can avoid registration with the SEC as investment advisers. The new legislation's recent amendments limit the availability of exemption relief for non–U.S. advisers, that is, more of them will be required to register. Thus, there has been a radical change from the earlier approach.

The method in which the number of clients a non–U.S. adviser will be decided is still unclear and will be clarified after additional studies and rulemaking; this pertains to the case when the adviser has a single investor who may invest in multiple funds sponsored by the same adviser, a trust with multiple beneficiaries, or an investment made through a joint account.

Unless there is another exemption available, non–U.S. advisers would have to register with the SEC under these conditions:

- The investment adviser should have more than 14 clients and investors in the United States in one or more private equity funds that it manages.

- Its assets worth $25 million or more should be attributable to the clients and investors in the United States.

- If non–U.S. advisers hold themselves out as investment advisers to the public, then they have to register with the SEC.

If the SEC increases the AUM threshold, the new private adviser exemption will provide limited relief from the SEC's registration requirements. The exemption will also limit the ability of non–U.S. investment advisers to raise funds in the United States without registering with the SEC.

As a registered adviser with the SEC, a non–U.S. investment adviser must maintain books and records; implement compliance programs; and develop and maintain a code of ethics, insider trading policies, and procedures.

If non–U.S. investment advisers have custody of clients funds, the advisers must arrange for review by independent public accountants registered with the Public Company Accounting Oversight Board. Non-U.S. investment advisers must adhere to additional reporting requirements.

They should report matters regarding the amount of AUM, use of leverage, counterparty credit risk exposures, trading and investment positions, types of assets held, side arrangements or side letters, valuation policies and procedures, trading practices, and any other information that is required by the SEC to assess systemic risk and protect investors.

The Dodd–Frank Act has its effects on non–U.S. advisers that advise U.S. and non–U.S. private funds with U.S. investors. Registration with the SEC will cause investment advisers additional compliance and administrative costs.

With the other economies of the world, such as Europe, Asia, and Latin America lagging behind in financial reform, the United States will face regulatory restrictive opportunities. This happens if these economies fail to adopt rules similar to those that have been created in the United States. It will take some time to iron out the details of the rules and regulations. Until that happens, the regulatory trends impacting both the United States and the global setup will face a great deal of uncertainty.

The European sovereign debt crisis has directly impacted the banking sector of both Europe and the United States. As there is no consensus on the peak default rates in certain products, uncertainty pervades the banking sectors of both continents.

The Basel Committee changes are being implemented a little slower than the other provisions and can bring about uncertainty, which can cause volatility in the markets. The Basel Committee is globally

responsive. It gets feedback on the proposals that are carried out successfully and those that are not all that successful. The Basel Committee has
an impact on global economies.

It impacts the ability of banks to raise certain amounts of capital,
credit, and credit flows in various economies. These impacts will have to
be well understood before the Basel Committee's global implementation.

The November 2010 G20 summit included financial reform in its
agenda. The G20 summit insisted that the Act's principles and standards
must encourage other nations to join the financial reform regime. The
G20 discussed the restrictions imposed by the Volcker Rule. Un-
fortunately, Korea, which had an advocacy on the issue, could not raise
its opinions, as it was the coordinator of the meeting.[1]

The Volcker Rule impacts domestic markets only on a short-term
basis. But when it comes to international financial markets, reduction in
proprietary trading may decrease foreign investments in local stock,
bond, foreign exchange, or derivatives markets. The recommendations
made in the G20 summit in response to the global financial crisis have
impacted regulatory developments in the last financial year.

The United States and Europe are divided in the policy approach
toward fiscal austerity measures and fiscal stimulus. There is a clear division in currency rate management, and the difference extends to financial regulatory reforms. A distinctive divide exists between countries
that favor and those that oppose the bank tax. The United States, the
United Kingdom, and Germany favor the bank tax; Canada, Brazil, and
Japan oppose the bank tax. These divides were clearly seen in the G20
Toronto summit in June 2010.

Investment Industry

Besides the banking industry, the Dodd–Frank Act impacts the investment management industry, affecting investment companies indirectly.
The SEC has a great deal of influence on mutual funds and their management. The Act will have to restructure the SEC and its management

so that the SEC can provide more effective oversight in the context of this regulatory framework.

The application of capital requirements to investment companies is highly unlikely. The prudential standards that are used in the regulation of banks hinder the normal operations of investment companies and their managers.

The Dodd-Frank Act does not have jurisdiction over mutual funds, but it establishes an Investment Advisory Committee under the SEC to address the issues related to investor protection and general SEC requirements.

The Act allows the SEC to bring enforcement actions against an investment company for breach of fiduciary duties. With its newly organized enforcement division, increased staffing, and ability of senior staff members to get tough, the regulation's ability to impact the investment company industry is increased.

There are requirements for registration and record keeping for private fund advisers. An investment in a private fund could be less risky than one in a mutual fund, as the compliance costs could be higher.

Instead of creating fiduciary standard provisions, the Dodd-Frank Act requires the SEC to conduct a study to evaluate the standards of care for broker-dealers and investment advisers. The SEC should also compare regulatory standards for broker-dealers with those for investment advisers.

The SEC should submit a report covering the regulatory gaps that negatively influence personalized investment advice about securities. The impact on brokers selling mutual funds depend on the rules adopted by the SEC.

In the future, the SEC should explore the financial literacy of retail investors, particularly regarding mutual fund shares. The study should be completed within two years. It should give information that retail investors would need to make informed financial decisions on mutual funds and also information regarding investments and conflicts of interests.

The Government Accountability Office is required to review and recommend improvements that to mutual fund advertising. This would help to improve investor protection. The SEC is required to establish point-of-sale disclosure rules for broker-dealers to provide basic information to retail investors before the purchase of an investment product or service. The SEC would have to hire 800 new employees as a result of the Dodd-Frank Act.

The Act establishes new rules to govern and regulate credit rating agencies. It changes the role of nationally recognized statistical rating organizations (NRSRO). The Dodd-Frank Act gives additional authority to the SEC by the creation of the Office of Credit Ratings (OCR). The OCR would create new requirements for the functioning and oversight of NRSRO. The changes brought about by these requirements would definitely affect money market funds.

Regarding derivatives, the Act brings about greater transparency and helps regulators to manage systemic risks and individual counterparties. The changes brought to the over-the-counter derivatives impact economies engaging in hedging transactions. This could impact investment strategies in both the long and the short term.

The SEC requires transparency of information regarding lending or borrowing of securities. It is not legal to lend or borrow securities outside the bounds of the new SEC rules. These rules could help independent directors in doing their duty to supervise securities lending.

The SEC is compelled to establish rules to direct national securities exchanges and national securities associations. This could lead to the prohibition of listing equity securities of an issuer that does not have an independent compensation committee. Although open-end mutual funds are not included in this requirement, closed-end mutual funds are included.

The Dodd-Frank Act expands the provisions in the Sarbanes-Oxley Act that are related to non-U.S. public accounting firms. With the new regulations of the Act, the fund industry would begin to experience see-through changes in individual business models, which could be assessed very conveniently by industry participants.

Although there are very few provisions regarding the registered fund industry, the impacts of those provisions will have great significance when implemented.

Summary

- The Dodd-Frank Act impacts many aspects of the banking industry, including capital requirements, returns, leverage, risk taking, transparency, and innovation.

- Given that other countries follow a universal banking model, they may be hesitant to implement the idiosyncratic restrictions of the Act.

- The Act raises the regulatory bar on a number of financial products, including mortgages and derivatives.

- The Act may have a number of unintended consequences, including fostering international inconsistency by allowing large financial institutions to fail and hedge funds to collapse.

- The Act's impact on non-U.S. investment advisers is significant, such as limiting the ability of nonregistered advisers to raise funds in the United States.

- Global markets face increased uncertainty as a result of the Act, Basel III, and the G20.

- The Act impacts the investment industry by empowering the Securities and Exchange Commission to bring enforcement actions, increasing compliance costs, and creating new regulations for credit rating agencies.

Note

1. www.koreatimes.co.kr/www/news/biz/2010/05/123_64751.html.

CHAPTER 8

Advice for Specific Professions

After reading this chapter, you will be able to:

- Understand the implications of the Dodd-Frank Act on executive management.
- Understand the Act's impact on municipal securities markets.
- Comprehend the ways in which broker-dealers will be impacted by the Act.
- Grasp the Act's implications for investment advisers.
- Understand how the act will impact insurers.

The Dodd-Frank Act is very comprehensive in scope. It has a potential impact on the operations and services of many streams of work. Due to this Act, more financial firms have hired compliance managers, accountants, lawyers, regulatory analysts, back-office professionals, software professionals, and information technology specialists.

Executive Management

Higher-level management of financial firms is impacted by the Dodd-Frank Act and has to plan properly in order to meet the changes brought by the Act. Management should concentrate on the votes on pay and on golden parachutes, independence of the compensation committee in public companies, and independence of the compensation consultant.

Compensation professionals will also have to pay attention to details regarding pay versus performance disclosure, the ratio of chief executive officer (CEO) compensation to that of an average employee, and mandatory claw-back provisions. Further, the professionals should lend their expertise to analyze the formal employee antihedging policy, limited broker voting, enhanced shareholder proxy access, and the disclosure of CEO's or chairperson's role in a company.

Compensation Committee and Its Independence

The Dodd-Frank Act mandates that the compensation committee of a public company should be independent. Members of the compensation committee should also be members of the board of directors. But this specification is not a requirement for controlled companies or limited partnerships. The independence of the compensation committee will depend on the source of the director's compensation and the director's relationship with the companies and their affiliates.

If a systemic financial company cannot comply with the Dodd-Frank Act, the company will be prohibited from being listed on the National Securities Exchange. The provisions of the Act specify that the Securities and Exchange Commission (SEC) should provide opportunities for covered companies to remove the defects that could result in their delisting.

Before selecting consultants, advisers, or legal counsel, a company's compensation committee should consider its independence. The compensation committee should have authority to retain a compensation consultant or adviser for the benefit of the company. The professionals hired should have project plans that can help them carry on with their work without facing adverse factors that emerge from material issues within the organization.

Say-on-Pay Vote

Shareholders should have a right to vote on the say-on-pay vote. They should have a say and approve the compensation of executive directors. This vote would be nonbinding, and it should provide a forum to oppose or support the company's compensation practices.

The "say on pay" is the most prominent driving factor of the compensation restructuring. It provides correlated perspectives regarding pay and corporate performance. Financial firms should first concentrate on creating a say-on-pay stakeholder team to review investors' past pay practices. The team should be able to define communication, plan structure, and performance metrics.

The independence of compensation consultants permits financial firms to perform something more than mere compensation consultancy.

Golden Parachute

The golden parachute excise tax would be applied to executive payouts when there is a change in the company's authority, as when stakeholders are asked to approve a merger, acquisition, consolidation, or proposed sale of company or its assets. The proxy in the documentation should disclose agreements with executives regarding transactions, amounts of compensation, conditions of payment, and so forth.

CEO-to-Employee Pay Ratio

The CEO-to-average-employee pay ratio should help the public company's top management to determine the compensation for all employees by using the SEC's Summary Compensation Table shown following.

Name and Principal Position	Year	Salary ($)	Bonus ($)	Stock Awards ($)	Option Awards ($)	Non-Equity Incentive Plan Compensation ($)	Change in Pension Value and Non-qualified Deferral Compensation Earnings ($)	All Other Compensation ($)	Total ($)
Principal Executive Officer									
Principal Financial Officer									
A									
B									
C									

Claw-Back Provisions

Public companies are required to implement claw-back policies under the Dodd-Frank Act. These policies should be able to determine the incentive-based compensation that would be paid to executives when there is material noncompliance with accounting standards that could result in misstatements thereby resulting in retracting money awarded as compensation to executives.

Municipal Securities Markets

The Dodd-Frank Act regulates certain unregulated participants that act as municipal advisers in the municipal market. The Act impacts the Municipal Securities Rulemaking Board (MSRB). The Act also establishes an Office of Municipal Securities within the SEC.

A municipal adviser is any person or entity that provides advice to or on behalf of a municipal entity or an obligated person and undertakes solicitation of a municipal entity with respect to financial products, investment advisory services, or issuance of municipal securities.

Guaranteed investment contract brokers, third-party marketers, financial advisers, solicitors, finders, swaps advisers, and placement agents are entities that are qualified to be considered as municipal advisers. Municipal entities and their employees, brokers, dealers, investment advisers who provide investment advice, municipal securities dealers who serve as underwriters, certain commodity traders, and attorneys who provide traditional legal services are not municipal advisers.

The Dodd-Frank Act prevents municipal advisers from engaging in malpractice. Municipal advisers are required to be registered with the SEC, and they should act in the best interests of the municipal entities they represent and for which they act as municipal advisers.

The Act requires the MSRB to promulgate rules that govern the advice given to municipal entities by municipal advisers. It also sets standards for municipal advisers. The MSRB is given the authority to reduce the regulatory burden that small municipal advisers face.

Office of Municipal Securities

The Office of Municipal Securities is a new division of the SEC. It will administer the SEC rules relating to municipal securities brokers, dealers, issuers, investors, and advisers. The office serves as a liaison between the SEC and the MSRB.

The Dodd-Frank Act requires certain studies to be conducted to ascertain the efficiency and adequacy of disclosure in the municipal securities market. The studies should evaluate the efficiency of repealing or amending the Tower Amendment, which limits the ability of the SEC or the MSRB to require a municipal securities issuer to make any filing with the SEC or the MSRB prior to the issuance of such securities.

Broker-Dealers

The Dodd-Frank Act imposes fiduciary duty on broker-dealers when they conduct businesses with retail customers. The Act empowers the Securities and Exchange Commission to impose the fiduciary standard. Investment advisers have a fiduciary duty to act in the best interests of clients. Unless broker-dealers charge separately for the advice they provide, they are required to comply with the fiduciary standard requirements.

The Act increases the number of measures that would cause fiduciary duties to be imposed on broker-dealers. The SEC will have to study the effectiveness of existing regulatory standards of care for brokers, dealers, investment advisers, and associated persons who provide investment advice.

The SEC should adopt rules that require broker-dealers to comply with the standards of conduct and to notify the retail customers and get their acknowledgment when broker-dealers provide a limited range of investment products.

The imposition of fiduciary standards on broker-dealers has impacted their business practices. Broker-dealers are required to disclose the capacity in which they deal with retail customers as principal or agents. They are not required to disclose their markup.

Broker-dealers are required to give notice to retail customers to provide consent or acknowledgment when they offer proprietary products. They should also ensure that their recommendations suit customers, as there is a wide gap between suitability and best interests of customers.

When the Dodd-Frank Act imposes fiduciary standards on broker-dealers for dealings with retail customers, it may complicate underwriters' ability to strike a balance between the issuers and purchasers in initial public offerings (IPOs). This eventually may lead to the exclusion of retail customers from the IPOs. Broker-dealers do not provide investment opportunities to all customers who have vested interests.

Investment Advisers

Investment advisers with an asset value of $100 million or more are required to register with the SEC. Some investment advisers are exempted from registering with the SEC. They are:

Non-U.S. Private Advisers

- They have place of business in the United States.
- Have fewer than 15 clients and investors in private funds in the United States.
- Have assets of less than $25 million under the management in the United States.
- Do not hold themselves to the public as investment advisers.

- Do not advise SEC-registered companies or business development companies.

Private Funds Advisers

- Solely advise private funds.
- Have less than $150 million of assets under the management in the United States.

Capital Funds Advisers

- Solely advise capital funds.
- Are required to keep records and provide SEC with reports to aid the SEC in protecting public interests and investors.

Mid-Sized investment advisers

- Have a consolidated asset value ranging from $25 million to $100 million.
- If these assets are registered in their home states, then they are subject to registration.
- Advisers to business development companies, SEC-registered investment companies, and those advisers who are required to register under the Registration Act are not exempted.

Family Offices

- The exemption must be consistent with the previous exemptive policy of the SEC.
- Based on the range of organizational, management. and employment structures employed by the family offices.
- Grandfather investment advisers to family offices that were not registered or not required to register under the Advisers Act of 2010.

Additional Exemptions

- Advisers registered with the Commodities Futures Trading Commission as commodity trading advisers that advise private funds.
- Advisers to small business investment companies.
- Intrastate advisers that do not advise private funds.

The provisions of the Dodd-Frank Act have implications on a broad variety of investment adviser activities. The legislation indicates that the investment adviser must not itself be a business development company. The Act bans certain banking entities from acquiring or retaining any equity, partnership, or any other ownership interest in a hedge fund or a private equity fund. The Volcker Rule may require banks to divest certain hedge funds and private equity funds.

The Dodd-Frank Act amends the definition of commodity trading adviser in the Commodity Exchange Act. The Act also makes certain security-based swaps "securities" and creates a fiduciary adviser role for those who would advise special entities swaps.

Insurers

Several provisions of the Dodd-Frank Act could help insurance companies and reinsurance companies to maintain their competitive positions in the global financial market, but the Act also can affect financial institutions, including insurance companies. The establishment of the Federal Insurance Office (FIO) should create a central point for insurance industry information.

The establishment on the new national underwriting standards for home mortgages would require lenders to verify borrower's income, credit history, and job status. The mortgage insurance companies would depend on the borrower's application information, and its validity would result in better operational results.

Insurance companies have used securitizations and derivatives to manage their risks, and the legislation has a marginal effect on these activities. But insurance entities with $50 billion in consolidated assets would be subjected to assessments on large financial companies. These assessments would help raise the $19 billion needed to offset some of the costs and expenses of the legislation's measures.

Insurance companies that are subject to the assessments are likely to make disbursements that are unrelated to the risks borne by the insurance industry. The absolute capital levels will also go down gradually.

If the U.S. financial regulatory system was to fail, U.S. reinsurers would be likely to face increased operational costs and lower profit margins. When capital costs increase, reinsurance cost could increase and the amount of reinsurance available to primary insurers could decrease. The FIO[1] would conduct a study and report to Congress on the modernization and improvement strategies that the insurance industry will require.

The insurance industry is rated according to the national and global competitive position of the insurers and on the quality and absolute levels of capital relative to the company's risk profile and sustainable earnings. Any changes to these rating factors could affect the ratings.

Summary

- Executive management will need to focus on the independence of the compensation committee, the independence of consultants and advisers, shareholders' "say on pay," and chief executive compensation and claw-back policies.

- The Dodd-Frank Act enhances the role of the Municipal Securities Rulemaking Board and establishes an Office of Municipal Securities within the Securities and Exchange Commission.

- The Act empowers the SEC to impose fiduciary duties on broker-dealers, which could impact initial public offerings.

- With some exceptions, investment advisers with assets of $100 million or more are required to register with the SEC.

- The Act contains several provisions that could help insurers maintain competitive positions in the global financial market.

Note

1. www.pciaa.net/web/sitehome.nsf/lcpublic/379/$file/Dodd-Frank_ Study_Deadlines.pdf

CHAPTER 9

Relationship with SOX and the Basel Accords

After reading this chapter, you will be able to:

- Understand the expanded whistleblower provisions of the Dodd-Frank Act.
- Recognize the incentives for publicly held companies to institute their own whistleblower programs.
- Understand how the Act works with the Basel Accord to reduce the probability of another systemic financial crisis.

The Dodd-Frank Act works with and enhances provisions found in the Sarbanes–Oxley Act and the Basel Accords. Working together, they facilitate stability and transparency and increase the likelihood of consumer protection.

The Dodd-Frank Act and SOX

The Dodd-Frank Act has worked its amendments into the Sarbanes-Oxley Act (SOX) and adds new private rights of actions for whistleblowers. It establishes a new whistleblower incentive program and has made several whistleblower-related changes to SOX.

The whistleblower incentive program requires the Securities and Exchange Commission (SEC) generally to pay a whistleblower in securities law action. Bounties ranging between 10% and 30% of the recovery will be paid by the SEC Investor Protection Fund. The SEC will not be able to pay the bounties in certain cases, as when the whistleblower is a member, officer, or employee of a certain regulatory body or government agency.

The Dodd-Frank Act prohibits employers from taking punitive actions against employees who: provide information to the SEC; assist the SEC in taking certain actions; and make disclosures that are protected under SOX, Securities Exchange Act, or a regulation subjected to the SEC. Employees whose rights are violated can file a complaint with the Department of Labor's Occupational Safety and Health Administration within 180 days from the date on which the violation has occurred or from the date on which the employee becomes aware of such a violation.

The Act states that any employee who holds claims under SOX has the right to a jury trial. SOX can openly prohibit the use of predispute arbitration agreements for claims. The Act has expanded the coverage for employees, covering employees of publicly traded companies, brokerage firms, contractors of publicly traded companies, nationally recognized statistically rating organizations, and subsidiaries of publicly traded companies.

The Act provides a private right of action for commodity whistleblowers and whistleblower protection for financial services employees. The legislation strengthens the antiretaliation provisions of the False Claims Act and requires the SEC inspector general to conduct a study on the whistleblower protections that come under this law.

The legislation has announced that the SEC will pay an award to those whistleblowers who report securities laws violations to it. If the whistleblower submits original information that is not known earlier by the SEC, then the SEC pays up to at least $1 million after enforcing its actions against the violators.

Penalties collected by the SEC will be used to pay whistleblowers 10% to 30% of the total sanction money received. Apart from this, whistleblowers will also get a portion of related fines collected by the U.S. Attorney General, state attorney general, and others. The implication is that public companies have a provision where an employee of a particular company can lodge a complaint against the violation of any security law, but the Dodd-Frank Act's provision has given whistleblowers an opportunity for a paid incentive as described above.

The Act could result in employees holding back relevant information in the early stages, when it could be reported to the company, because employees intend to report the original information to the SEC at a later date for a large incentive payment. This could leave company management at a disadvantage because of the lack of critical data. Hotline programs that are now in effect have emphasized the principle of anonymity. The hotline services offered are independently administered, and employees who submit information have their identities hidden, which aids in the exposure of frauds and other violations. By these services, public company management can act quickly to save money and enjoy more benefits.

Most progressive organizations have adopted the concept of employee reporting and have incorporated hotlines into their enterprise-wide risk plans, which include audit findings, certification exceptions, and reports of risky behavior from other sources. Public company codes of conduct list what actions are wrong, and employees are offered training courses on how to report information.

The required knowledge is imparted through intranet Web sites, newsletters, pay stubs, and so on. A lot of time and effort has been invested in hotlines to ensure their efficiency.

The Dodd-Frank Act must reinforce the core values of public companies and must inform employees and partners of these companies of the importance of telling the company when its code of conduct is violated. The provision in Section 922 of the Act on whistleblower protection does not inhibit the effectiveness of hotlines.

The Dodd-Frank Act and the Basel Accords

The Dodd-Frank Act and the Basel Accords jointly have the capacity to reduce the probability of the occurrence of a financial crisis. In addition, they can limit the severity of a financial crunch's repercussions. They have been designed to make sure that banks hold enough capital to withstand losses during periods of recession and can carry out their activities without turning to taxpayers for help. Both the Act and the Accords are designed to ensure that major financial institutions are subject to careful and consistent capital requirements.

These standards strengthen banks, have more capacity to absorb losses, and facilitate a stable and resilient financial system. Both the Basel Accords and the Dodd-Frank Act give enough time to government agencies and thereby financial institutions to agree to the new capital requirements that would help directly in the economy's recovery. The systemic financial institutions are also subject to stricter regulations related to equity ratios.

Although the Dodd-Frank Act applies to banks that have a consolidated asset value of over $50 billion, the Basel Accords have not yet specified size requirements. Even with the Act displacing too-big-to-fail, financial institutions do not have the necessary incentives to supervise their own capital.

The Basel Accords take rating agencies' credit ratings and risk-weighted assets (RWAs) very seriously. The Accords rely heavily on ratings of external rating agencies to assign risk weights to various exposures. The Dodd-Frank Act has shown interest in removing these agencies from performing regulatory duties. The divergence of ratings agencies has caused disagreements between the Dodd-Frank Act and Basel Accords.

The Basel Accords and the Dodd-Frank Act both protect taxpayers by limiting the risk taken by their financial institutions.

Summary

- The Dodd-Frank Act has expanded upon the whistleblower provisions of the Sarbanes-Oxley Act of 2002, providing whistleblowers with financial incentives in actions brought by the Securities and Exchange Commission.

- Employers are prohibited from taking punitive action against whistleblowers; employees whose rights are violated can file a complaint with the Department of Labor.

- The SEC's incentive program may have the unintended consequence of employees withholding information from employers.

- Due to increased capital requirements, the Act and the Basel Accords lessen the likelihood of a global financial crisis.

Contents of the Dodd-Frank Act

Section 1. Short title; table of contents

Section 2. Definitions

Section 3. Severability

Section 4. Effective date

Section 5. Budgetary effects

Section 6. Antitrust savings clause

TITLE I: FINANCIAL STABILITY

Section 101. Short title

Section 102. Definitions

Subtitle A: Financial Stability Oversight Council

Section 111. Financial Stability Oversight Council established

Section 112. Council authority

Section 113. Authority to require supervision and regulation of certain nonbank financial companies

Section 114. Registration of nonbank financial companies supervised by the Board of Governors

Section 115. Enhanced supervision and prudential standards for nonbank financial companies supervised by the Board of Governors and certain bank holding companies

Subtitle B: Office of Financial Research

Subtitle C: Additional Board of Governors
Authority for Certain Nonbank Financial Companies
and Bank Holding Companies

TITLE II: ORDERLY LIQUIDATION AUTHORITY

TITLE III: TRANSFER OF POWERS TO THE COMPTROLLER OF THE CURRENCY, THE CORPORATION, AND THE BOARD OF GOVERNORS

Subtitle A: Transfer of Powers and Duties

Subtitle B: Transitional Provisions

TITLE IV: REGULATION OF ADVISERS
TO HEDGE FUNDS AND OTHERS

TITLE V: INSURANCE

Subtitle A: Office of National Insurance

Subtitle B: State-Based Insurance Reform

PART I: NONADMITTED INSURANCE

TITLE VII: WALL STREET TRANSPARENCY AND ACCOUNTABILITY

Subtitle A: Regulation of Over-the-Counter Swaps Markets

PART I: REGULATORY AUTHORITY

Section 711. Definitions

Section 712. Review of regulatory authority

Section 713. Portfolio margining conforming changes

Section 714. Abusive swaps

Section 715. Authority to prohibit participation in swap activities

Section 716. Prohibition against Federal Government bailouts of swaps entities

Section 717. New product approval CFTC—SEC process

Section 718. Determining status of novel derivative products

Section 719. Studies

Section 720. Memorandum

PART II: REGULATION OF SWAP MARKETS

Section 721. Definitions

Section 722. Jurisdiction

Section 723. Clearing

Section 724. Swaps; segregation and bankruptcy treatment

Section 725. Derivatives clearing organizations

Section 726. Rulemaking on conflict of interest

Section 727. Public reporting of swap transaction data

Section 728. Swap data repositories

Section 729. Reporting and recordkeeping

Section 730. Large swap trader reporting

Section 731. Registration and regulation of swap dealers and major swap participants

Section 732. Conflicts of interest

Section 733. Swap execution facilities

Subtitle B: Regulation of Security-Based Swap Markets

TITLE VIII: PAYMENT, CLEARING, AND SETTLEMENT SUPERVISION

TITLE IX: INVESTOR PROTECTIONS AND IMPROVEMENTS TO THE REGULATION OF SECURITIES

Section 901. Short title

Subtitle A: Increasing Investor Protection

Section 911. Investor Advisory Committee established

Section 912. Clarification of authority of the Commission to engage in investor testing

Section 913. Study and rulemaking regarding obligations of brokers, dealers, and investment advisers

Section 914. Study on enhancing investment adviser examinations

Section 915. Office of the Investor Advocate

Section 916. Streamlining of filing procedures for self-regulatory organizations

Section 917. Study regarding financial literacy among investors

Section 918. Study regarding mutual fund advertising

Section 919. Clarification of Commission authority to require investor disclosures before purchase of investment products and services

Section 919A. Study on conflicts of interest

Section 919B. Study on improved investor access to information on investment advisers and broker-dealers

Section 919C. Study on financial planners and the use of financial designations

Section 919D. Ombudsman

Subtitle B: Increasing Regulatory Enforcement and Remedies

Section 921. Authority to restrict mandatory pre-dispute arbitration

Section 922. Whistleblower protection

Section 923. Conforming amendments for whistleblower protection

Section 924. Implementation and transition provisions for whistle-blower protection

Section 925. Collateral bars

Section 926. Disqualifying felons and other "bad actors" from Regulation D offerings

Section 927. Equal treatment of self-regulatory organization rules

Section 928. Clarification that section 205 of the Investment Advisers Act of 1940 does not apply to State-registered advisers

Section 929. Unlawful margin lending

Section 929A. Protection for employees of subsidiaries and affiliates of publicly traded companies

Section 929B. Fair Fund amendments

Section 929C. Increasing the borrowing limit on Treasury loans

Section 929D. Lost and stolen securities

Section 929E. Nationwide service of subpoenas

Section 929F. Formerly associated persons

Section 929G. Streamlined hiring authority for market specialists

Section 929H. SIPC Reforms

Section 929I. Protecting confidentiality of materials submitted to the Commission

Section 929J. Expansion of audit information to be produced and exchanged

Section 929K. Sharing privileged information with other authorities

Section 929L. Enhanced application of antifraud provisions

Section 929M. Aiding and abetting authority under the Securities Act and the Investment Company Act

Section 929N. Authority to impose penalties for aiding and abetting violations of the Investment Advisers Act

Section 929O. Aiding and abetting standard of knowledge satisfied by recklessness

Section 929P. Strengthening enforcement by the Commission

Section 929Q. Revision to recordkeeping rule

Subtitle C: Improvements to the Regulation of Credit Rating Agencies

Section 966. Suggestion program for employees of the Commission

Section 967. Commission organizational study and reform

Section 968. Study on SEC revolving door

Subtitle G: Strengthening Corporate Governance

Section 971. Proxy access

Section 972. Disclosures regarding chairman and CEO structures

Subtitle H: Municipal Securities

Section 975. Regulation of municipal securities and changes to the board of the MSRB

Section 976. Government Accountability Office study of increased disclosure to investors

Section 977. Government Accountability Office study on the municipal securities markets

Section 978. Funding for Governmental Accounting Standards Board

Section 979. Commission Office of Municipal Securities

Subtitle I: Public Company Accounting Oversight Board, Portfolio Margining, and Other Matters

Section 981. Authority to share certain information with foreign authorities

Section 982. Oversight of brokers and dealers

Section 983. Portfolio margining

Section 984. Loan or borrowing of securities

Section 985. Technical corrections to Federal securities laws

Section 986. Conforming amendments relating to repeal of the Public Utility Holding Company Act of 1935

Section 987. Amendment to definition of material loss and nonmaterial losses to the Deposit Insurance Fund for purposes of Inspector General reviews

Subtitle J: Securities and Exchange Commission Match Funding

TITLE X: BUREAU OF CONSUMER FINANCIAL PROTECTION

Subtitle A: Bureau of Consumer Financial Protection

Subtitle B: General Powers of the Bureau

Subtitle C: Specific Bureau Authorities

Subtitle D: Preservation of State Law

Subtitle E: Enforcement Powers

Subtitle F: Transfer of Functions and Personnel; Transitional Provisions

Section 1066. Interim authority of the Secretary

Section 1067. Transition oversight

Subtitle G: Regulatory Improvements

Section 1071. Small business data collection

Section 1072. Assistance for economically vulnerable individuals and families

Section 1073. Remittance transfers

Section 1074. Department of the Treasury study on ending the conservatorship of Fannie Mae, Freddie Mac, and reforming the housing finance system

Section 1075. Reasonable fees and rules for payment card transactions

Section 1076. Reverse mortgage study and regulations

Section 1077. Report on private education loans and private educational lenders

Section 1078. Study and report on credit scores

Section 1079. Review, report, and program with respect to exchange facilitators

Section 1079A. Financial fraud provisions

Subtitle H: Conforming Amendments

Section 1081. Amendments to the Inspector General Act

Section 1082. Amendments to the Privacy Act of 1974

Section 1083. Amendments to the Alternative Mortgage Transaction Parity Act of 1982

Section 1084. Amendments to the Electronic Fund Transfer Act

Section 1085. Amendments to the Equal Credit Opportunity Act

Section 1086. Amendments to the Expedited Funds Availability Act

Section 1087. Amendments to the Fair Credit Billing Act

Section 1088. Amendments to the Fair Credit Reporting Act and the Fair and Accurate Credit Transactions Act of 2003

Section 1089. Amendments to the Fair Debt Collection Practices Act

TITLE XI: FEDERAL RESERVE SYSTEM PROVISIONS

TITLE XII: IMPROVING ACCESS TO MAINSTREAM FINANCIAL INSTITUTIONS

TITLE XIII: PAY IT BACK ACT

TITLE XIV: MORTGAGE REFORM
AND ANTI-PREDATORY LENDING ACT

Subtitle A: Residential Mortgage Loan Origination Standards

Subtitle B: Minimum Standards For Mortgages

Subtitle C: High-Cost Mortgages

Section 1431. Definitions relating to high–cost mortgages

Section 1432. Amendments to existing requirements for certain mortgages

Section 1433. Additional requirements for certain mortgages

Subtitle D: Office of Housing Counseling

Section 1441. Short title

Section 1442. Establishment of Office of Housing Counseling

Section 1443. Counseling procedures

Section 1444. Grants for housing counseling assistance

Section 1445. Requirements to use HUD-certified counselors under HUD programs

Section 1446. Study of defaults and foreclosures

Section 1447. Default and foreclosure database

Section 1448. Definitions for counseling-related programs

Section 1449. Accountability and transparency for grant recipients

Section 1450. Updating and simplification of mortgage information booklet

Section 1451. Home inspection counseling

Section 1452. Warnings to homeowners of foreclosure rescue scams

Subtitle E: Mortgage Servicing

Section 1461. Escrow and impound accounts relating to certain consumer credit transactions

Section 1462. Disclosure notice required for consumers who waive escrow services

Section 1463. Real Estate Settlement Procedures Act of 1974 amendments

Section 1464. Truth in Lending Act amendments

Section 1465. Escrows included in repayment analysis

Subtitle F: Appraisal Activities

Section 1471. Property appraisal requirements

Section 1472. Appraisal independence requirements

Section 1473. Amendments relating to Appraisal Subcommittee of FFIEC, Appraiser Independence Monitoring, Approved Appraiser Education, Appraisal Management Companies, Appraiser Complaint Hotline, Automated Valuation Models, and Broker Price Opinions

Section 1474. Equal Credit Opportunity Act amendment

Section 1475. Real Estate Settlement Procedures Act of 1974 amendment relating to certain appraisal fees

Section 1476. GAO study on the effectiveness and impact of various appraisal methods, valuation models and distributions channels, and on the Home Valuation Code of conduct and the Appraisal Subcommittee

Subtitle G: Mortgage Resolution and Modification

Section 1481. Multifamily mortgage resolution program

Section 1482. Home Affordable Modification Program guidelines

Section 1483. Public availability of information of Making Home Affordable Program

Section 1484. Protecting tenants at foreclosure extension and clarification

Subtitle H: Miscellaneous Provisions

Section 1491. Sense of Congress regarding the importance of government-sponsored enterprises reform to enhance the protection, limitation, and regulation of the terms of residential mortgage credit

Section 1492. GAO study report on government efforts to combat mortgage foreclosure rescue scams and loan modification fraud

Section 1493. Reporting of mortgage data by State

Section 1494. Study of effect of drywall presence on foreclosures

Section 1495. Definition

Section 1496. Emergency mortgage relief

Effective Dates and Deadlines

Dodd-Frank Effective Dates/Rules Promulgation Deadlines

Provision	Notes	Title	Effective Date	Rule or Required Action	Compliance Date
General effective date		Sec. 4	1 day after date of enactment (unless otherwise indicated)		
FRB/FDIC Joint Final Rules on Resolution Plan	The FRB and FDIC are to jointly issue final rules on the requirements of resolution plans	I Sec. 165(d)(8)		18 months from enactment	
FRB Rules on Risk Committees	FRB to issue final rules on risk committee requirements	I Sec. 165(h)(4)		1 year after "transfer date" (i.e., 1 year after enactment subject to extension of up to 6 months	
FRB Title I Final Rules	FRB is to issue final rules implementing Title I (other than OFR issues)	I Sec. 168		18 months from enactment	
Court Rules for Expedited Liquidation Proceedings	Courts required to establish rules for expedited liquidation proceedings	II Sec. 202(b)(1)		6 months from enactment	

Provision	Notes	Title	Effective Date	Rule or Required Action	Compliance Date
Federal Insurance Office (FIO)	Federal insurance office to be established	V Sec. 4 of bill	1 day after enactment		
Nonadmitted and Reinsurance Reform Act		V Sec. 512	12 months after enactment	2 years after enactment, states must participate in uniform national insurance producer database	
Source of Strength Rules	If an insured depository institution is not the subsidiary of a bank holding company or savings and loan holding company, the appropriate Federal banking agency for the insured depository institution shall require any company that directly or indirectly controls the insured depository institution to serve as a source of financial strength for such institution	Vi Sec 616 (d)	Effective on the transfer date to the appropriate federal regulator	The appropriate federal banking agencies shall jointly issue final rules to carry out this section.	Not later than 1 year after the transfer date to the appropriate federal regulator
Volcker Rule (Proprietary Trading)	FSOC to make recommendations on implementation, including how to "accommodate business of insurance" implementation regulations	VI Sec. 619	Earlier of 12 months after regulation promulgated or 2 years after enactment	Within 6 months of enactment within 9 months of release of FSOC study (above)	2 years from promulgation of final rules (potential of 3 additional 1-year extensions)
Regulation of Over-the-Counter Swaps Markets	CFTC will regulate swaps and related activities. SEC will regulate security-based swaps and related activities	VII	On the later of 360 days after the date of enactment, or to the extent rulemaking is required, not less than 60 days after publication of the final rule or regulation		

(*continued*)

Provision	Notes	Title	Effective Date	Rule or Required Action	Compliance Date
Bureau of Consumer Financial Protection (BCFP)	New consumer financial protection bureau established to regulate financial companies for market conduct (insurers exempt except for FCRA enforcement)	X Sec. 1062 Sec. 1100G	"Transfer Date" must be at least 180 days, but not more than 12 months after enactment, 12 months (extensions up to 18 months possible)	Treasury Secretary must set the "Transfer Date" within 60 days of enactment	
Incentive-based compensation	Appropriate federal regulators to prescribe regulations/guidance for disclosure of incentive-based compensation arrangements	IX Sec. 956		9 months after enactment	
Mortgage Reform and Anti-Predatory Lending Act	BCFP to enforce existing and new consumer mortgage laws and regulations	XIV Sec. 1400	Not later than 12 months after issuance of final regulation	18 months after the transfer date in Title X (BCFP)	

© 2010 Property Casualty Insurers Association of America, www.pciaa.net/web/sitehome.nsf/lcpublic/379/$file/ Dodd–Frank_Effective_Dates.pdf

Glossary of Key Acronyms

BCFP (Bureau of Consumer Financial Protection)   This is a new office created by the Dodd-Frank Act. This office assumes the consumer protection responsibilities from several preexisting entities that already exist, such as the Federal Trade Commission. Once the transition is complete, the office will regulate a wide variety of consumer financial services as well as high-interest payday loans.

BHC (bank holding company)   This is an entity or company that controls one or more banks. By becoming a BHC, a traditional bank is able to raise its capital easily. It can assume the debts of shareholders to borrow money, to acquire other banks and nonbanking entities, and to issue stock. Bank holding companies are regulated not only by the Securities and Exchange Commission but also by other branches of the government.

BHCA (Bank Holding Company Act)   This Act regulates the actions of bank holding companies. Enacted in 1956, this Act requires Federal Reserve Board approval for the establishment of a bank holding company and prohibits bank holding companies headquartered in one state from acquiring a bank in another state.

CDFI (Community Development Financial Institution)   This institution provides credit and financial services to markets and populations that remain underserved in the U.S. economy. A CDFI may be a community development bank, a community development credit union, a community development loan fund, a community development venture capital fund, a community development corporation, or a micro-enterprise development loan fund.

CDS (credit default swaps)   A CDS is a kind of counterparty agreement that allows transfer of third-party credit risk from one party to another. It is designed to transfer the credit exposure of fixed income products between parties.

CFTC (Commodities Futures Trading Commission)   This independent agency was created to protect market users and the public from fraud, manipulation, and abusive practices related to sale of commodities and financial futures, and fosters open, competitive, and financial sound futures and option markets.

ECOA (Equal Credit Opportunity Act)   Enacted in 1974, this law makes it unlawful for any creditor to discriminate against any applicant with respect to any credit transaction. This law applies to any person who participates in a credit decision.

EESA (Emergency Economic Stabilization Act)   This law was enacted in 2008 in response to the subprime mortgage crisis.

Foreign Banking Organization (FBO)   Foreign banking organizations can acquire or establish freestanding banks or bank holding companies in the United States. These entities are regulated and supervised as domestic institutions.

FCRA (Fair Credit Reporting Act)   This Act, enacted in 1971, regulates the collection, dissemination, and use of consumer information, including consumer credit information. Companies that gather and sell the credit information are called consumer reporting agencies (CRAs). The information that CRAs sell to creditors, employers, insurers, and other business is called a consumer report.

FDIC (Federal Deposit Insurance Corporation)   This corporation was created by the Glass-Steagall Act of 1933. It examines and supervises certain financial institutions, performs certain consumer protection functions, and manages banks in receiverships. It provides deposit insurance that ensures the safety of deposits in member banks. Currently the safety limit of deposits in member banks is up to $250,000 per depositor per bank.

FHFA (Federal Housing Finance Agency) This independent agency came about as a result of the merger of the Federal Housing Finance Board and the Office of Federal Housing Enterprise Oversight.

FINRA (Financial Industry Regulatory Authority) FINRA is the largest independent regulator for all securities firms doing business in the United States. We oversee nearly 4,620 brokerage firms, 165,920 branch offices and 636,340 registered securities representatives. Our chief role is to protect investors by maintaining the fairness of the U.S. capital markets.

FIO (Federal Insurance Office) This office monitors the financial industry and coordinates the industry policy. It does not have regulatory authority. It aims at expanding the federal level knowledge of state-related insurance regulation issues.

FMU (Financial Marketing Utility) An entity that manages a multilateral system for clearing, transferring, or settling payments, securities, or other financial transactions.

FRA (Federal Reserve Act) This 1913 Act created the Federal Reserve System, the central banking system in the United States, and granted it the legal authority to issue legal tender.

FRB (Federal Reserve Board) This governing body of the Federal Reserve System monitors the economic health of the country and sets Federal Reserve policy regarding the discount rate and reserve requirements.

FSOC (Financial Stability Oversight Council) This council was created by the Financial Stability Improvement Act. It oversees banks and nonfinancial banks in material distress. It identifies risk to the financial stability of the country.

GAO (Government Accountability Office) This nonpartisan agency does auditing and evaluation programs and activities for the Congress. It is an investigative arm of Congress charged with examining matters relating to the receipt and payment of public funds.

GLBA (Gramm-Leach-Bliley Act) This Act, enacted in 1999, lifted the restrictions on banks that offer commercial banking, insurance, and investment services. It is also known as the Financial Services Modernization Act.

HFSC (House Financial Services Committee) This committee oversees the entire financial services industry, including securities, insurance, banking, and housing industries. It also oversees the work of the Federal Reserve and other financial service regulators.

HMDA (Home Mortgage Disclosure Act) This Act, passed in 1975, requires financial institutions to maintain and disclose annually data about home purchases, home purchase preapprovals, home improvement, and refinance applications.

MSP (Major Swaps Participant) A major swap participant is defined as anyone that maintains a substantial net position in swaps, exclusive of hedging for commercial risk, or whose positions creates such significant exposure to others that it requires monitoring.

MSRB (Municipal Securities Rulemaking Board) This board creates investor protection rules and other rules that regulate broker-dealers and banks in the municipal securities market.

NAIC (National Association of Insurance Commissioners) Formed in 1871, this nonprofit organization organizes the regulatory and supervisory efforts of the various state insurance commissioners.

NRSRO (Nationally Recognized Statistical Rating Organization) This agency issues credit ratings permitted by the Securities and Exchange Commission. The credit ratings are used by financial firms for regulatory purposes.

OCC (Office of the Comptroller of Currency) This office was established by the National Currency Act of 1863. It charters, regulates, and supervises all national banks and federal branches and agencies of foreign banks in the United States.

OFR (Office of Financial Research)   This office enables financial regulators to understand complex financial products. It helps to uncover frauds, monitors risks, and oversees the critical linkages between the important institutions in the financial market.

SAFE Act (Secure and Fair Enforcement for Mortgage Licensing Act)   This Act requires all mortgage loan originators to register with the Nationwide Mortgage Licensing system (NMLS) to satisfy the prelicensing education. It implements stricter laws and regulations in real estate and mortgage.

SBA (Small Business Administration)   Established in 1953, this government agency provides support to small businesses. It assists in the economic recovery of communities after disasters.

SBC (Senate Committee on Banking, Housing and Urban Affairs)   This committee has jurisdiction over banking, economic policy, financial institutions, price controls, deposit insurance, and economic stabilization.

SBIA (Small Business Investment Act)   This Act was enacted in 1958. It was created to encourage small business programs, such as businesses for minorities, women-owned businesses, and start-up businesses.

SBIC (Small Business Investment Company)   This company provides equity capital and long-term loans subsidized by the Small Business Administration. It may lend money or buy stock or convertible debentures in firms that hold a consolidated value of assets less than $5 million.

SEC (Securities and Exchange Commission)   This commission regulates securities markets and protects investor interests. It also monitors corporate takeovers. It promotes full public disclosure and protects against fraudulent practices in the securities market.

SRO (self-regulatory organization) This is a nongovernmental organization that has the authority to create and enforce industry regulations and standards. It protects investors' interests, establishes rules, and promotes ethics and quality.

TARP (Troubled Asset Relief Program) This government program was created for the establishment and management of a Treasury fund to curb the financial crisis that occurred in 2007–2008. It gives the Treasury purchasing power to buy mortgage-backed securities from institutions all over the country.

TILA (Truth in Lending Act) This Act was established in 1968. It was designed to protect customers in credit. It promotes informed use of consumer credit, gives consumers the right to cancel certain credit transactions, and with the exception of certain high-cost mortgage-loans, it does not regulate the charges that are imposed for consumer credit.

About SOX Institute and the GRC Group

Training Programs and Professional Certifications

As the recognized global leader in governance, risk, and compliance, the GRC Group offers professionals a comprehensive knowledge repository and widely acclaimed training and certification programs in:

- Sarbanes-Oxley
- Governance, Risk Management, and Compliance
- Information Security and Information Technology Governance, Risk, and Compliance

Through its SOX Institute and GRC Institute, the GRC Group provides unsurpassed peer-to-peer learning opportunities, world-class instruction, and access to cutting-edge research and materials. GRC Group members are leaders in their fields, and those with certifications deliver unprecedented value to their employers.

Join the GRC Group today and receive a wealth of benefits, including:

- Free webinars
- Training seminar discounts
- Discounted admission to conferences and symposia
- Subscription to the *Inside GRC Journal*
- Access to audio recordings and slides of archived webinars

Visit www.grcg.com to join today!

Index